Praise for
Just Keep Growing

"*Just Keep Growing* reads like a beautifully curated gallery of leadership insights—each chapter a different canvas, layered with personal stories, reflections, and practical takeaways. Martha explores the nuances of servant leadership with the same care an artist brings to composition. It's an inspiring guide for leaders and creatives, and anyone looking to shape meaningful experiences." **–Ethan Reed, veteran Disney Imagineer, toy designer, author, and illustrator**

"In her introduction, the author makes a number of promises–about compassion and community, humor and healing, purpose and practicality, stewardship and service–for the developing leader and seasoned servant leader alike. She fulfills every one of them. A heartfelt and inspiring book." **–Linda W. Belton, author and retired healthcare executive**

"Martha Boehm offers us 25 great places to start–or re-start–a servant leadership journey. The stories are interesting and inspiring, and they are followed by questions for reflection and specific suggestions for action. Reading this book is a great way to just keep growing!"
–Kent M. Keith, CEO Emeritus of the Greenleaf Center for Servant Leadership and author of *Servant Leadership at Work: Caring About People and Getting Extraordinary Results*

"Martha has written a book that is a must–read for anyone who wants to understand servant leadership from the inside out. She is a spirit carrier who poetically and thoughtfully engages our hearts, minds, and souls by telling the stories of other spirit carriers with wit and wisdom, goodness and grace." **–Tom Thibodeau, distinguished professor of servant leadership, founder of Viterbo University's master of arts in servant leadership, and part owner of a country tavern**

"This is a beautiful book—full of stories, by turns humorous and poignant, illuminating a key truth of servant leadership: lasting influence comes not just from what you do but from who you are." **–Richard Kyte, author and director of the D. B. Reinhart Institute for Ethics in Leadership at Viterbo University**

"Vibrant, accessible stories make servant leadership come alive. Augmented by memorable three-word phrases, thought-provoking questions, and practical advice, *Just Keep Growing* helps all of us become better humans."
–Sister Sarah Hennessey, Franciscan Sisters of Perpetual Adoration (FSPA), and a spiritual director at the Franciscan Spiritual Center

"*Just Keep Growing* is a warm book of relatable stories. You will find great wisdom from regular people working through common problems with uncommon courage, durability, and insight. Easy to learn from with a clear pathway to apply the learnings for the greater good."
–Jeff Thompson, former CEO of Gundersen Health System, retired pediatrician, and author

Just Keep Growing

25 Servant Leadership Lessons

Martha Boehm

Fox Bamboo Press

Cover design by Martha Boehm

Ayan (2016) reprinted with permission from James A. Bowey. F.I.E.R.C.E. 5 Method reprinted with permission from Carolyn Colleen.

Printed in the United States of America.

Library of Congress Control Number: 2025907300

ISBN: 979-8-9985498-0-9 (Paperback)
ISBN: 979-8-9985498-1-6 (eBook)

Fox Bamboo Press
La Crosse, Wisconsin

To my first servant leaders,
my parents, John and Barbara Boehm,
and to leaders with and without a fancy job title.

CONTENTS

Preface

I noticed my part-time coworker sitting by herself in the hallway. She seemed a bit down, so I sat next to her.

"Hey, how's it going?" I asked. She said she was struggling and that things seemed to be building "like a multitiered cake."

"Have you tried to push it over?" I asked.

"Yes, it's too heavy," she responded.

"Have you tried shoving your face in it? You know, try a different approach."

She briefly paused and then started laughing. Hard.

I joined in. Her laughter was contagious. The hallway instantly filled with joy. We both pictured the same thing: a funny mess. Then we went our separate ways.

I saw her a week later. She told me our short conversation was "like the best therapy." When something somewhat stressful happened later that afternoon, she said, "It didn't make the cake." In other words, she was not going to let it build and bother her.

Several months passed. In fall, she stopped by my office to say hello at the beginning of her shift. We hugged and briefly caught up.

"Have you shoved your face into any cakes lately?" I asked. She laughed.

We remembered where we were sitting when we had that initial conversation. While I knew our short time together in that hallway was helpful for her, I didn't know just how much until she told me that day. She said she realized the multitiered cake that had been building in her mind wasn't as big, rigid, or scary as she had feared. She thought it was going to be hard, but when she fell into a fake-baked cake, she felt relieved.

"It was like giving myself permission to release my exhaustion," she said.

She realized not all of her worries were worth it. Things started to get better when she reframed the situation, allowed herself to fully fall forward, and found an imaginative way to start breaking down the stressful layers that had been building. It always amazes me how laughter and imagination can help us sort stressful situations.

We will further explore how humor can heal later in this book. It's one of 25 relatable short stories that teach a lesson on servant leadership, a style of leadership that prioritizes the needs of followers and emphasizes personal integrity and growth in a safe and supportive environment. Robert K. Greenleaf coined the phrase *servant leadership* in the 1970s, explaining that "it begins with the natural feeling that one wants to serve, to serve *first*. Then conscious choice brings one to aspire to lead."[1] Servant leaders should be observant, curious, and trustworthy. They make sure people grow in different ways.

As Greenleaf pointed out:

> The best test, and difficult to administer, is this: Do those served grow as persons? Do they, *while being served*, become healthier, wiser, freer, more autonomous, more likely themselves to become servants? *And*, what is the effect on the least privileged in society? Will they benefit or at least not be further deprived?[2]

We can do this by being active listeners, encouraging self-care, and asking generative questions that give life.

I wrote this book for people who want to be known as compassionate and confident leaders who take care of the people they serve. Young adults starting their career will benefit from this work as they determine the type of leader they want to be. People who are placed in positions to lead a team will benefit from this work as they navigate the various needs of their followers. Established leaders will also benefit from this work as they are reminded about the benefits of lifelong learning. At the end of each chapter, you'll find reflection questions and action items. You'll quickly discover servant leadership is practical, and you'll be able to apply the lessons learned to your personal or professional life. This book will help people become better leaders at home and/or away as they build on their strengths, understand the value of systems thinking, and create a healthy and safe environment.

I will show you how stories reveal purpose, provide ways to approach difficult conversations and build common ground, and recommend a practical method to make ethical decisions. We will explore our sphere of influence and be reminded of the importance of community. As you progress through the book, you will hopefully start asking, "How do you know?," discover what's on your heart, and learn the benefits of letting your mind wander. I will recommend tools for overcoming adversity, address ways to solve system glitches, and explore how to be good stewards of our resources. We will discuss gratitude and mindfulness, the importance of finding light in your life, and ways to support rising leaders.

This book has given me the opportunity to combine different aspects of my career in journalism, communications and marketing, and leadership. I've learned you don't need a particular job title to be a servant leader; you need to be an active listener, to accept constructive feedback, and to be open to change. I have had opportunities to lead throughout my life, including as the captain of my high school swim and softball teams, as a member of a planning committee and task force, as an evening storyteller, as a student and teacher in the classroom, as a swim instructor, as a lifeguard, as an announcer for a 5K race, as a volunteer in a community garden, as an event planner, as an usher at a theater, as an actress on stage, as a host parent to an international high school exchange student, as a coworker with an open office space, as a speaker, and as a beloved family member. Some of the stories that follow are personal. Some are from interviews with people I admire. Some are from mass media that inspire me. All of the stories are real, relatable, and relevant.

When I was an intern at a TV station in Milwaukee, an anchor encouraged me to title all of my stories in just three words. He said if I can do that, I have narrowed my focus, and my writing should be crisp and concise. The following stories capture attention, create emotional connections, and make lessons memorable. Each chapter features a different situation, but the concepts build upon each other. While gathering story ideas and writing the chapters, I tried to be mindful of representation and include people of different backgrounds, professions, cultures, colors, religions, ages, sexes, and genders.

I earned a master of arts in servant leadership from Viterbo University. To remember what I learned from each class, I would write my Top 5 Takeaways—three words for the theme, followed by a few explanatory sentences. When I completed the program, I had more than 50 takeaways. For my graduate colloquium project, I decided to take what I considered my Top 10 Takeaways at the time and create stories that exemplify the lessons. I've now expanded that project into this book, with 25 chapters that I feel not only exemplify servant leadership lessons but encourage readers to make personal and professional connections to the work.

I hope you take away whatever you need from this book, whether it's learning something new, being reminded of a certain topic's importance, or healing from a past hurt. I hope this book is "like the best therapy" for you. Greenleaf encourages us, "No matter how difficult the challenge or how impossible or hopeless the task may seem, *if you are reasonably sure of your course, just keep on going!*"[3] Additionally, I believe we have to **just keep growing**.

CHAPTER 1

Go Beyond Transactions

The excitement level was high. The temperature was low. It was a perfect December day for Green Bay Packers football in Wisconsin. Kickoff was just two hours away. Dave couldn't wait to drive his wife and two guests to the game. His friends had never been to Lambeau Field. At 10 a.m., they checked out of their hotel. While walking to the car, Dave realized the keys were in his jacket, which was locked in the trunk.[4]

"Talk about embarrassing," Dave said.

It was too cold to walk two miles to the game. They could have called a cab, but one might have been hard to come by so close to game time and the cost would likely have been inflated. Rideshare services like Uber and Lyft did not exist yet.

Dave told the hotel's guest services the situation. They called their locksmith, who arrived about 15 minutes later.

"If you want to get to the game in time, I'm going to have to do some damage to your trunk," the locksmith said.

Dave told him to go ahead. Two rather aggressive hits with a rubber mallet later, the trunk popped open. Dave picked up his jacket and held the misplaced keys. He paid the locksmith and drove to the stadium. While he enjoyed the game, he couldn't help but think about his keys. The drive home sparked a memory of a time a guest at one of his family-owned grocery stores had a similar experience. Dave Skogen is the chairman of the board of Skogen's Festival Foods.

"I'm going to call a locksmith," Dave declared. "I want to see how much it'll cost us to have them come out on an as-needed basis."

A partnership formed with a local locksmith company in La Crosse, Wisconsin. At just one grocery store, a locksmith serviced one car a month. They had four stores at the time. The partnership and service expanded as their grocery business grew across the state.

"We can afford this," Dave said. "This will help bring the customer back. This is just part of our culture."

In general, grocery store owners are focused on transactions. Depending on the size of the store, there could be tens of thousands of items scanned daily. It's important to have high-quality products at a competitive price and an overall positive shopping experience. Dave went beyond the transaction by turning a stressful personal experience into a complimentary service for customers. Going beyond transactions is about building relationships and creating a positive experience that ultimately creates loyal customers/guests. Dave further emphasized that Festival Foods' culture, their higher purpose, is "in serving and enriching the lives of others."[5]

Going beyond the transaction—in any industry—will be what sets you apart.

Horst Schulze is the founder, chairman, and CEO of the Capella Hotel Group and the former president of the Ritz-Carlton Hotel Company. He notes there are three things all people who are served want: the product or service to be free of defects, timeliness, and people to be nice to them.[6] If an experience can be individualized and personalized, that's even better, he further explained. This can be as simple as acknowledging someone's presence.

Pat was 38 years old with Down syndrome. His mother, Sally, said he was often ignored when they were out in public, but a young, part-time Festival Foods bagger named Jesse specifically talked to Pat. They talked about the Packers and had a short conversation.

"Pat was just beaming as we drove away," Sally wrote in a letter to the store manager. "I did thank Jesse as we left, but just wanted to let you know how that young man made my son's day." Dave contacted Sally to thank her for her letter, which was read during a Festival Foods morning employee huddle at that store and across the state. It lifted Jesse up, emphasized the importance of kindness and small talk with strangers, and helped build the company culture. About seven years ago, Pat died. Dave and his son went to the funeral.

As companies work to increase transactions and focus on profits, oftentimes it can feel as though requests are made, tasks are completed, and we quickly move on. We need to work on building relationships and making stronger connections with the people who request and complete tasks. We should find ways to thank individuals for specific things, not just give blanket thank-yous to continue to encourage them. We need to **go beyond transactions**.

Reflection Questions
1. How can you tell an interaction was a transaction?
2. How can we build relationships to go beyond the transaction?
3. Why is it important to focus on relationships?

Action Items
1. Describe a situation in which you experienced a transaction. Think about ways you can go beyond it.
2. Write an example of an automated telephone call you've experienced when asking a company for help. Then write how the system can be improved.
3. This week, when you're running an errand, take note of how someone goes beyond a transaction. Write down what they did and how they created a relationship.

CHAPTER 2

Stories Reveal Purpose

Fourteen-year-old Tom skipped two days of basketball practice so he could plan his ten-year-old brother's birthday party. Tom sent invitations, made a barbecue dinner, and baked cupcakes. He got streamers to decorate, planned the games, and bought a bike as a gift.[7] Their mother used to do the party planning, but, unfortunately, she was dealing with deep postpartum depression after having her sixth child and was placed in a psychiatric unit. Their father wasn't able to help with the party planning due to work obligations that kept him late at the office. Tom never started another basketball game. His coach had benched him for missing practice without an explanation. Mental illness is hard to talk about today, much less in 1962. Tom felt like there wasn't a supportive structure in place to tell his coach about his mother and how he had to support his family in new ways. It wasn't until later in life that Tom Thibodeau, distinguished professor of servant leadership, revisited some of his life stories. That's when he noticed patterns related to prayer, service, and community. It's also when he realized **stories reveal purpose**.

Tom's mother was on bed rest during the last three months of her pregnancy. Her bed was moved to the family living room. That's where she taught Tom, the oldest son, to cook, clean, iron, and sew. When she went into postpartum depression, Tom dropped out of school for a short time. He was in sixth grade.

"I have these vivid memories of caring for my family," Tom said. "I gave my brothers haircuts. My mother was a beautician. She had haircutting equipment, and I gave them haircuts, and they were terrible haircuts. Just terrible," he said with a laugh.

Tom's father had asked members of their Catholic church to help care for the kids. He wanted them to keep going to the same school and to be able to pick everyone up and go to mass together on Sunday.

"We all had to go and live with different families, and we never talked about it," Tom explained. "But now, as adults, we're starting to have these conversations, and it's just amazing because we all grew up in different families, having different experiences, and therefore with different burdens to carry."

Tom didn't talk much about his experience until after he turned 60. As a child, Tom had been placed with a family who had a boy who was a year older than him and a younger sister. The boy seemed to be in trouble a lot with his dad, who would often come up to their room at night and yell at him.

"I felt so terribly alone," Tom remembered. "And one night, he got yelled at, and I was lying in my bed, which was right next to the window. And I looked out at the moon and the stars, and I just started to pray from my heart, 'Dear God, please take care of my mom and my dad. Please, dear God, bring my family back together.' And I felt this amazing sense of warmth. I kinda felt like I was loved. So, at 12 years of age, I became a person of prayer."

Later that week, Tom was riding in the car with his dad. He asked him who was taking care of his mom. "A team of psychologists and psychiatrists," his dad answered. Tom wanted to know what you had to do to become one of them. His dad told him he'd need a master's degree in counseling to become a psychologist and to go to medical school to be a psychiatrist.

"At age 12, I decided to be a person of service. I wanted to help people like my mother who are suffering."

When Tom was in high school, his mother was in and out of psychiatric units. No one asked him about his mother. People didn't know what to say, so they didn't say anything—at least directly to the kids. However, members of the community were working on ways to help. Every day, Monday through Friday, a different casserole would be dropped off at their house.

"The community fed us, took care of us."

Tom earned a bachelor's degree in psychology and English and earned a master's degree in counseling and social ministry.

After college and grad school, Tom worked as a lay minister in British Columbia. He returned to western

Wisconsin to work with children with mental and emotional disabilities and then spent most of his career as a teacher. He started part-time at Viterbo College (later University) in the Department of Religious Studies. He also worked with the Upward Bound Program—a federal program from the President John F. Kennedy administration that assisted first-generation college students—at the University of Wisconsin–La Crosse, and he taught reality therapy courses for teachers at a college in Chicago. He helped start Viterbo University's master of arts in education and later its master of arts in servant leadership, after resisting the administration's desire for a pastoral ministry graduate program.

"It should include people from every walk of life, from every religious denomination," Tom told Viterbo's president. "It fits with our mission and who we are. This belongs to the community."

As Herbert Anderson and Edward Foley wrote in their book, *Mighty Stories, Dangerous Rituals: Weaving Together the Human and the Divine*, "The stories we tell, whether human or divine, mythic or parabolic, order experience, construct meaning, and build community."[8]

Everybody has a story to tell. Stories connect us to each other and help us build compassion and empathy for our fellow humans. Stories provide a structure and help us heal. **Stories reveal purpose.** By reflecting on his past and telling stories about different times in his life, Tom was able to see patterns. He started to feel a

greater sense of purpose—which was gradually revealed—and better understand all of the ways he has
been able to help people in different life circumstances
thanks to his personal experiences.

"It's kind of amazing how at age 12 things kind of
got set in motion," Tom said. "As I look back on my life
and the pattern that it's taken, my life has always been
rooted in prayer, service, and community. And those are
my core beliefs. And so, if I find myself in a situation or
in a group that doesn't respect those three aspects, those
three virtues, I can't do my best work."

Since 1996, his work has also included caring for
people at The Place of Grace, a Catholic worker house.
Now, at 74 years old, Tom doesn't know what his future
holds—none of us really do. He doesn't know how his
story will end. He understands there's a mystery to that,
to live in the unknown. But what's no longer a mystery
to Tom is that "our lives are both sacred and social."

"I keep going back [to the fact] that my mother's
mental illness, her postpartum depression, was the greatest gift she could have given me. And I've come to understand deeply that suffering without love is intolerable.
Love without suffering is sentimental. Love with suffering is redemptive."

Reflection Questions

1. In what ways do you reflect on significant moments in your life and their deeper meaning?
2. With whom have you shared your sacred stories?
3. How can you tell you're fulfilling a purpose?

Action Items

1. Tell a story about a significant moment in your life. Explain how the story reveals purpose.
2. Reflect on a goal you've achieved. List the ways it positively impacted your life and added deeper meaning.
3. Consider joining a committee or organization in which you support its mission or vision to feel like you're fulfilling a greater purpose.

CHAPTER 3

Rituals Are Powerful

We were told, if we laughed, it would be disrespectful, and we would not be able to stay. While we were just barely teenagers, we took that statement seriously. Our chosen leader, Brad, stood ahead of our 40-person group. We waited in silence on a large grassy field. Across from us were three women and three men at the entrance to a white building with red trim and intricate carvings. Two of the men ran toward us. One held a small dagger; the other held a large spear. They were bare-chested and barefoot and wore grass skirts. At times, they would stop and swing their weapons, chant something indistinguishable to us, stick their tongues out, and open their eyes wide. After swinging his spear close to our leader, the second man dropped to one knee. While making direct eye contact with Brad, he placed a small fern branch in front of him. The man took a few steps back, pointed his spear at it, and made a few loud vocal sounds. Brad walked forward slowly. He picked up the branch, made eye contact with the man with the spear, and stood still. Picking up the branch meant we came in peace. The man swirled the spear close to his body several times, turned away from us, slapped his right hand on his right thigh, and retreated across the field to the building. The man with the dagger did the same. The three women and remaining man who stood by the building started to sing, chant, and move their bodies in unison. This was all part of a *pōwhiri*, a Māori welcoming ceremony. We were now able to walk forward and enter the marae, or meeting house, in Rotorua, New Zealand.

It was quite a memorable welcome! When we first arrived on the property, a woman came on our bus and said, "Kia ora," a Māori phrase for "Hello, welcome, and greetings." She explained how we would be "welcomed in formal order" and Brad's important role in representing our People to People Student Ambassador Program group. Had we not been briefed on what to expect, I likely would have been a bit alarmed, intimidated, or worried about staying overnight. And there's the potential I would have laughed out of discomfort or confused wonderment. The welcoming ritual could appear to be quite an aggressive challenge or threat if you didn't understand the tradition. After getting settled in the marae and following the rules—no shoes, no photos, and no stepping on pillows—we had dinner with our new friends. They prepared hāngī, a traditional dinner of roasted pig and potatoes cooked for about four hours underground using the unique geothermal properties of the area. We were told this ritualistic meal is usually prepared in the spirit of hospitality for weddings, ceremonies, christenings, and funerals.

After dinner, we watched *kapa haka*, traditional Māori performing arts. They began with *waiata-ā-ringa*,

or action songs with gentle hand movements accompa-
nied by guitar. Members of our group were then called
on stage for a *poi* performance. I was given two *poi* and
shown how to use them. I held a cord in each hand and
somewhat skillfully but not simultaneously twirled balls
in small, round circles. Our group also performed a few
songs and asked for their participation. Before we all
parted ways, we stood in a large circle, held hands, and
repeated the words to the song "Now Is the Hour."[9] We
said goodbye with another ritual, a *hongi*. We shook
hands and gently pressed our noses together, signifying a
strong connection and meeting on a spiritual level.

Watching my VHS tape and reading my journal
jogged my memory and provided trip details. I couldn't
help but smile at my young self and reflect on the signif-
icance of this trip of a lifetime to New Zealand and Aus-
tralia. It sparked my love of international travel, and
while I don't think the word *reverence* was used at the
time, I learned about its importance, especially for traditions that are different from my own.

In his book *Reverence: Renewing a Forgotten Virtue*,
Paul Woodruff wrote, "Reverence is the well-developed
capacity to have the feelings of awe, respect, and shame
when these are the right feelings to have."[10] Rituals can
bring us together or tear us apart. We need to make sure
our heart is in the right place and be deliberate when we
celebrate. Reverence keeps ceremonies from being
empty.[11] Had any one of us laughed at the *pōwhiri*

welcoming ceremony, we would not have been welcomed in the marae, we would not have been able to share a traditional meal, we would not have been able to share our musical talents with each other, and we would not have been able to form a strong connection and understand the strength, love, and kindness of the Māori people.

I am reminded about this cultural travel experience when I watch a haka. After winning a gold medal at the Paris 2024 Olympic Games, the New Zealand women's rugby team performed a haka. Similar to the *pōwhiri* we witnessed, a haka usually includes stomping of feet, rhythmic body slapping, loud chants, protruding tongues, and the incorporation of traditional weapons. For Māori, a haka is a ceremonial war dance or challenge that represents pride, strength, and unity.

It takes time and practice to reach an understanding about what emotion is right during a particular moment and when something feels right or wrong. It's about patience, understanding, and respect. Habits are automatic, process driven, and mindless. Rituals are intentional, purpose driven, and mindful.[12] **Rituals are powerful.** Rituals may include celebrating personal and professional milestones, holidays, and successful endeavors. The virtue of reverence helps servant leaders to create a safe and supportive environment where people of different cultures are welcome—where various rituals and celebrations are respected and can be honored in the way they were intended—and to provide an opportunity to build community.

Reflection Questions
1. What are some of the rituals in your family?
2. How do you know when you need to have reverence toward a situation or ceremony?
3. What are rituals in different parts of the United States?

Action Items
1. Describe a ritual you've seen at work. Why is it important to the company culture?
2. Research a ritual in a country other than the United States. Describe the ceremony and how people act.
3. Review rituals in your family or create a new one.

CHAPTER 4

Celebrate Third Places

I was swimming under the sea when I started laughing so hard I couldn't sing. It was my first time on stage wearing my giant blue fish costume for La Crosse Community Theatre's October 2015 production of Disney's *The Little Mermaid*. My foam and fabric costume was so big that it had changed my upper body choreography. I couldn't get my arms high enough to match what the human me had been doing in rehearsals. I also had to pay more attention to my surroundings, as my fishtail exponentially extended the length of my backside. As we ran through "Under the Sea"[13] during dress rehearsal, I got caught in my castmate's colorful sea anemone costume. It made me laugh even harder as I wiggled away at the end of the scene, drawing Ariel's unexpected attention. It was a moment of pure joy that the directors noticed. We made that moment look planned during the run of the show, and it got a good laugh from the audience. I still think fondly of that show and the connections I made with others at the Weber Center for the Performing Arts, "a third place" where I built social capital.[14]

In his book *Celebrating the Third Place: Inspiring Stories About the "Great Good Places" at the Heart of Our Communities*, Ray Oldenburg explained that a third place is a location "in which people relax in good company and do so on a regular basis" outside of their home or work, which are first and second places, respectively.[15] The Weber Center is a third place where multiple generations can make friends, experience impactful storytelling, and feel safe expressing themselves on and off stage. During theatrical productions, the cast, crew, and production team learn to depend on each other. Sometimes that's in the form of helping each other learn lines, assisting with costume changes, or making sure we're all on the same page—quite literally before we are "off book" and need everything memorized.

Other third places may include running clubs, fitness facilities, ice cream parlors, coffee shops, churches, national parks, neighborhood cul-de-sacs, bowling alleys, American Legion posts, and family farms. These "great good places" build friendships, strengthen connections, and serve communities. Investing in community is how, according to political scientist Robert Putnam, we build social capital—more trust in society and an increased openness to connect and collaborate. As he notes in his book *Bowling Alone: The Collapse and Revival of American Community*, "the core component of social capital, as we use the term, is social networks; and the core insight of social capital theory is that social networks have value, both for people in the networks and for bystanders."[16] Online platforms like Facebook groups and other virtual communities can also be considered third places if administrators have positive intent to serve the common good and are mindful of the type of impact they are making on- and offline.

According to Putnam, growing social capital can increase our "educational performance, safe neighborhoods, equitable tax collection, democratic responsiveness, everyday honesty, and even our health and happiness."[17] I am fortunate to have met incredibly creative, compassionate, and community-minded people who have improved my quality of life. For example, some of my "mersisters" (from Disney's *The Little Mermaid*) and I get together a few times a year to catch up. During another performance, I made fast friends with one of the other actors. We occasionally play board games together with our husbands. We need to identify and **celebrate third places** for bringing joy, fostering friendships, and creating collective community experiences.

Reflection Questions
1. What are some third places that you've experienced in your community?
2. What has been the most meaningful part of having a third place for you?
3. How can you lift up great good places and their benefits in your community?

Action Items
1. Tell the owner/coordinator of a third place how much the organization means to you. This could be in the form of a card or letter, an intentional "thank you" the next time you attend an activity, or offering to host an upcoming event.
2. Think about how you can build social capital at your organization. Bring ideas to an upcoming committee meeting or start discussing opportunities with your department or division.
3. When was the last time you talked to your neighbor(s)? Be more intentional in making contact that can further foster a third place where you live.

CHAPTER 5

Sphere of Influence

Latin Grammy nominee and award-winning musician Gina Chávez loves rhythm. It's one of the foundations of her music. She loves percussive instruments, especially the guitar because of its chord progression and how it flows when she's strumming it. She enjoys working with the rhythm of words as a songwriter. That can be challenging due to different ways to portray lyrical emotion. For example, when recording her hit "La Que Manda," or "The Woman in Charge," Gina wanted to find just the right way to portray that she used to bury her dreams and now she doesn't; she's "the boss."[18] She recorded about 30 different versions that were missing that magic rhythm.

"I tried thinking my way through the song," Gina said. "I didn't know what to do. So I just told my producer, 'Roll the track. I'm just going to scream. It's not going to be pretty. I have no idea what's going to come out.'"[19]

What came out was a visceral call, or anthem, to listen to your heart and believe in yourself.

"When I'm songwriting, I have to constantly remember the lessons of what that song taught me," Gina said. "And I don't really feel like it came from me. It's more that it came through me. And I think the best songs I've written I've allowed to come in that way."

The beauty of music is that rhythm and lyrics allow for individual interpretation and help connect people across the world. Gina hopes her music and philanthropic work uplift and inspire others. After spending a year teaching English on a mission trip in Soyapango, El Salvador, Gina and her wife, Jodi, created a college fund program called Niñas Arriba, which means "Girls Rising." The program helps young women who have overcome many different hardships attend a private, Catholic university. Gina and Jodi have supported the young women by asking about their dreams, helping them build upon their strengths, and allowing them to form a community among themselves where they can further encourage each other. For example, Gina asked Vanessa, or Vane, about her career goal. She noticed Vane's interest in fitness and suggested she consider being a trainer. Vane responded that she wants to be a life coach.

"And I was like, 'Oh my God! 100%. You would be a perfect life coach,'" Gina said.

Their conversation advanced to discussing how they could work that goal into part of the college fund program. Vane was able to encourage and inspire her peers, not only by helping them exercise and eat healthier but also by using her words and taking action. Vane has since graduated from college and still partners with Niñas Arriba to help young women in her community.

"What I've learned is we all have a **sphere of influence**," Gina said. "You have a sphere of influence that I don't have. You know people I don't know. You have sway with people I don't have sway with. You don't have to be big and famous. Every single one of us has a sphere of influence that's particular to them."

Gina tours internationally as a cultural ambassador with the U.S. State Department. As a singer-songwriter, she has a sphere of influence through her music and at her concerts. Gina loves to be on stage and belt out her songs. But she also loves connecting with people at the merchandise table during intermission and after the performance. Audience members usually tell her their favorite part of the show, who they brought to the concert, or how far they traveled.

"Inevitably, people share incredibly beautiful things about their lives or something that they're taking away from that event," Gina said.

There is one particular moment that has stayed with Gina for years. After a performance in North Carolina, a teenager who had helped the event sound crew visited Gina and the band backstage. He showed her a note on his phone.

"He had written, 'I'm gay too.' And I'll never forget that," Gina said. "He couldn't even say it. And it just made me realize that (a) representation does matter and (b) what a blessing it is to have people in professions where they stay. I get to travel, do my thing, and leave.

I'm not there for that kid every day. It was beautiful to be able to be there in that moment and give him a hug and tell him, 'It gets better.' I also realize we need people who stay, who can support each other."

Gina emphasized the importance of educators—like her wife, who works as a vice principal—who support students and their families on a daily basis. She also noted the importance of mentors and supportive community members who just want the best for people. Our humanity is what connects us on the deepest level.

"Our ability, our capacity for loving other people, is directly correlated to our capacity to love ourselves," Gina said. "There will not be peace in the world until there is peace inside each one of us."

We have to think more deeply about how our words and actions impact others. Reaction is the opposite of contemplation. There are plenty of ways the world can knock us down and things can go wrong. We need to find opportunities to build each other up and to encourage and inspire others. We also have to be kind to ourselves and be grateful for the gifts we've been given and the opportunities that are still out there. If you're looking for inspiration, listen to music and lyrics that encourage you to believe in yourself, dare to dream, and remember we all have a **sphere of influence**.

Reflection Questions
1. Who are you most influenced by?
2. Who do you influence the most in your personal and professional life?
3. How could you make improvements to the words you use daily, whether having an internal conversation or talking to others?

Action Items
1. Describe a situation in which words either empowered you or knocked you down. Explain how you felt and if you would change your reaction based on more self-reflection.
2. Write a letter to yourself. Describe your strengths, how you accomplished a goal, and a dream you still want to achieve. Focus on encouraging words and gratitude for the gifts you've been given.
3. Identify organizations in your community that are focused on supporting and uplifting others.

CHAPTER 6

Begin with Good

Two large vases are filled with beautiful, fresh flowers. They have been placed on two stools on stage. Fully opened hot pink roses draw attention. Smaller light pink roses, spider mum spray, and bluebells accompany them. The bouquets are accented by unopened daylilies, greenery, and baby's breath. Collectively, they give an aura of wild elegance.

"I chose these flowers on purpose because most of these flowers that are growing in here are actually almost like wildflowers," Broadway actor Arbender Robinson said. "There aren't many flowers you will only see in a forest, but some of these you will see growing in the peace gardens where I spent my morning as part of my own restoration for today."[20]

Robinson has appeared in an impressive list of Broadway shows, with his debut being the Tony Award–winning production of *Hairspray*[21] and his most recent *The Book of Mormon*.[22] He was also a part of the cast of the revival of *Les Misérables*,[23] where he covered Marius and became the first African American to play the role on Broadway.[24]

When Robinson is asked to speak at various events, he surrounds himself with "tiny, tiny miracles."[25]

"That's why there are flowers here," Robinson said. "I think flowers are like millions of miracles happening here. So take a look. Enjoy them."

Robinson is also sure to wear a colorful bow tie and fun socks during his presentation.

"So no matter what happens today, at least I had on a cute bow tie, and I wore fun socks. So I win!"

The enamored audience responded with applause and laughter. Robinson's enthusiasm was infectious. He also expressed his gratitude for being able to share his story. Expressing gratitude is a way of focusing on the good, which can be done in several ways.

Dr. Amit Sood spent 10 years developing his gratitude practice. He is the creator of the Resilient Option program, which focuses on stress management and mindfulness well-being.

He is also the executive director of the Global Center for Resiliency and Wellbeing and a retired professor of medicine at Mayo Clinic. His work has focused on resilience and well-being, with research on the design of the brain, its struggle with focus and fatigue, and ways we can try to maximize happiness.

"Think about three of the most important people in your life," Sood advised during a presentation on resilient living.[26] "When you wake up tomorrow, before you leave the bed, think of these three people. Send them your silent gratitude for them being in your life."

The practice takes about two minutes. Sood recommended going one person at a time—or one pet at a time, since they are part of the family—thinking about something they said or did that was good.

"Assume you're protecting them for the week by sending them gratitude," he said.

Appreciation could also come in the form of a random text message during the day, a sticky note on a bathroom mirror, or a prayer.

Sood's gratitude practice can be applied at work as well. If colleagues are anticipating a tense meeting or phone call, Sood recommends meditating on the people you'll talk to soon.

"Preemptively plan gratitude," he said.

That's what Robinson does in his personal life and before he goes on stage. Near the end of his presentation, he asked the audience what they had learned from the conference.

"Joy in the presence of people," a man in the third row shouted in response. Robinson was excitedly intrigued and asked him to further explain.

"I'm trying to figure out, Why is he more joyful than me?" the man responded, referring to Robinson's infectious energy and charismatic stage presence.

"It's about taking all of my nervous energy and making it positive," Robinson responded with increased enthusiasm. "My mother taught me that."

Robinson suggested, like Sood's gratitude practice, finding a way to pause and reflect. He does so by starting his day by writing until he fills three pages.[27]

"Prayers are usually answered in that moment," he said. "That's one way I force or allow myself to simply slow down."

When we're not feeling particularly joyful, Robinson suggested taking what we've learned on our journey and moving forward by hitting the reset button. **Begin with good.**

Reflection Questions
1. What is one thing that's going good for you?
2. What do you need in order to focus on good things going on in your life?
3. How can you start meetings at work that focus on good things happening with a project, in your department, or at your organization?

Action Items
1. Come up with one specific thing you'll do to practice gratitude daily, such as journaling, meditating, or exercising.
2. Designate a time each day to practice gratitude.
3. Wear a favorite piece of clothing for an important meeting or presentation. Think about the particular meaning it has for you.

CHAPTER 7

Have Courageous Conversations

An older man walked into a funeral home with his wife and son. He wasn't ill; he had just reached an age in which he thought he needed to make arrangements. He wanted to feel in control of his end-of-life decisions.

"I knew him, knew the family," retired funeral home director Dean Dickinson said. "The old man is a tire kicker, and he came through the door with an attitude and basically told me, in so many words, this is what he's going to do and there's going to be minimalization and 'none of this funeral stuff.' Clearly, he didn't consider the feelings of his family, including the grandchildren, in his plans."[28]

"I don't want to buy a casket," the man said.

"You don't have to buy a casket," Dickinson explained. "You can have a funeral service and rent a casket, and after the service is over, we'll cremate the body just like you want."

Dickinson explained that his experience providing services to families had confirmed for him the value in creating a situation that allows for those grieving the loss of a loved one to spend time with the deceased before final disposition—how the body is handled after death—regardless of whether that disposition is a burial, an entombment, or a cremation. He said kids especially want to see Grandpa, for example, as part of processing that he's gone.

The man and his wife decided to look at caskets on the selection floor. The prices were transparent. Renting a casket was half the cost of buying one.

"Take your time," Dickinson said. "I'll stop back and see how you're doing."

About 10 minutes later, after sensing they had made a choice, he returned. The man and his wife had chosen to rent two of the more expensive caskets available for their services. They worked with Dickinson to make the rest of the arrangements and went on their way. About three years later, the man died. All of the prearrangements were put into play. Only 15 minutes after the family arrived for the service, the widow asked to talk to Dickinson.

"My husband and I talked many, many times about whether you sold us a bill of goods," she said. "But everything is playing out just the way you said it. The grandkids are up there [by the casket], and they're talking to their grandpa, and they're talking to each other. I want to thank you."

This situation played out many times for Dickinson in his 30-plus years as a funeral home director assisting families through the funeral process. Dickinson had been part of the funeral industry since he was a kid. His parents bought a funeral home in La Crosse, Wisconsin, in 1955. Early in his life, Dickinson harbored no desire to be a funeral director. His inclination was to be a chef or pursue a career in the U.S. Navy and travel the world. When Dickinson was 10 years old, he would come home at lunch to help his dad move caskets from a storage area at the end of the selection room. After school, he'd help move them back. At age 12, Dickinson went on his first death call with his dad. A couple of years later, he worked the front door at visitations. By 18, he'd gone on his first death call on his own. He graduated from the University of Minnesota's Program of Mortuary Science. After serving in the Vietnam War, he returned home and co-owned the funeral home with his brother. They worked to expand the service area to meet the needs of the community. At the time of this writing, Dickinson Family Funeral Homes and Crematory is owned and operated by Dean Dickinson's two nephews.

"It isn't easy for those of us who understand and appreciate the ritualization of the experience that provides a benefit to those grieving a loss," Dickinson said. "To be worthy of the procession in which we serve, we must provide that guidance. Counseling isn't argumentative or confrontational but focuses on the needs of the family even as they might have a preset attitude that is more characterized by avoidance. Families come to understand the only way out is through. There's no shortcut through the grief experience."

Everyone grieves differently and may have a different emotional reaction to the news of death or when someone receives a certain prognosis. Some people will work through anticipatory grief, having a greater amount of time to process a death versus experiencing a more shocking, sudden death. Some people may have been grieving a long time before coming to the funeral home for the service. It's not easy to talk about death and grief, but we need to have courageous conversations and to talk about tough topics.

Language is the primary way we communicate with our community. We can lift each other up just as easily as we embarrass or dehumanize others. Socrates said it is the greatest good to discuss virtue every day.[29] Courage is a cardinal virtue. In times of crisis, courageous people evaluate the situation and find the best way to move forward.[30] It's courageous to talk about difficult situations, to give feedback, and to propose solutions for the common good. What impacts us personally impacts us professionally. Whether we are assisting family members after the death of a loved one, letting an employee go, or working through a project led by a poor manager, we need to find the courage to speak the truth with love.

If we can **have courageous conversations** early in life about difficult topics, it becomes a bit easier to process information, to understand how things may progress, and to work through changes on a physical, emotional, and spiritual level. Although it's a natural human desire to want to feel in control of our lives, we never really know what will happen in the future. We can work through stages of life and grief together if we're courageous enough to discuss them openly and honestly with people we trust.

Reflection Questions
1. Why are certain topics difficult to discuss?
2. How do you approach a tough topic?
3. In what ways can you establish trust and understanding, the foundations of courageous conversations?

Action Items
1. Make a list of topics that are difficult for you to talk about. Write the emotions you feel when you think about the topics.
2. Choose a tough topic that you want to discuss. Meet with a trusted family member or friend and start the conversation. Or start a journal entry and just write what you're thinking.
3. Consider seeking a counselor or spiritual director if you feel there is something in your life that you have trouble talking about that impacts your daily way of living.

CHAPTER 8

Reach Common Understanding

Every day, six friends meet at Jim's Café for lunch. They come for lively conversations, a sense of community, and comfort food in the form of giant onion rings and big burgers. Since they dine so frequently, the restaurant staff have placed a small, plastic tabletop sign to designate the group's spot as the "Table of Knowledge."[31] The lighthearted designation refers to the wisdom the retired men have gained over the years and their many topics of conversation.

During their lunch, one of the Table of Knowledge diners received a phone call. He pulled his flip phone out of his pocket and answered.

"I'm in a big meeting," he said in a somewhat serious tone. His friends laughed. He smiled. "Call me later if you can. Thank you."

Additional laughter filled the restaurant, including that of television host and writer Phil Rosenthal. He had been visiting with the group as part of his Netflix travel documentary series, *Somebody Feed Phil*.[32] As Rosenthal dined with the Table of Knowledge as part of the "Mississippi Delta" episode in season 4, he learned that almost all of the men either were born in the town of Greenville, Mississippi, or had lived there for 50–60 years. Rosenthal asked them about their conversations. One man responded that some of them have political differences.

"But you're all still friends, and you're all eating lunch together every day," Rosenthal said in response. They nodded as they chowed down on their food.

"We agree to disagree and be agreeable about it," another man responded.

So often, our society tends to focus on what divides us instead of what unites us. When we share a meal together, we have an opportunity to build trust and relationships and find common ground. We can see different perspectives and ask generative, life-giving questions beyond the common, and often shallow, "How are you?" When we get to know each other on a deeper level, we tend to be more patient and understanding.

My father-in-law, Joe Furlano, is fortunate to meet with three of his friends once a week. Every Tuesday, they eat breakfast at a local restaurant. One of Joe's tablemates was initially an acquaintance. They became friends through their weekly breakfast meetings. While Joe always orders the "early bird special," the conversation varies from the success of sports teams, to family activities, to reminiscing about old times. Joe served in the U.S. Air Force. Another friend served in the U.S. Army. Two of the frequent diners worked together decades ago. While the retirees may joke that they gather weekly because they get hungry and want to simply get out of the house, they really go because they respect and care about each other. Similar to the Table of Knowledge, Joe and his friends have built trust and understanding by simply listening to each other. They have been building common ground for years.

According to Richard Kyte, the director of Viterbo University's D.B. Reinhart Institute for Ethics in Leadership, we tend to disengage and feel angry and defensive if we're not listened to, we're easily dismissed, or we feel like the discussion goes in unproductive circles.[33] Oftentimes, that's because we're not working through the same set of reasoning. Kyte notes that once we see others are being rational, reasonable solutions will present themselves even if we're not happy about the outcome.

Usually, the outcome after a meal together with friends is a belly full of food and laughter. As witty episodes of *Somebody Feed Phil* show us, dining with different cuisines and cultures challenges us to keep an open mind and help us **reach common understanding**. We can do so one meal at a time.

"It doesn't matter how you open a mind," Rosenthal said in between bites of food. "Sometimes you gotta open a mouth first, and the mind will follow."[34]

Reflection Questions
1. How often do you share a meal with family and friends?
2. What kind of topics do you discuss when you have lunch or dinner?
3. How have you reached common understanding on a divisive topic?

Action Items
1. Share a meal with a classmate, a coworker, or an acquaintance.
2. Add a budget line item for team lunches or simply schedule a time for everyone to eat together as a team bonding activity or to celebrate a win.
3. Watch an episode of *Somebody Feed Phil* as a family or with a friend. Discuss cultural differences and how we can reach common understanding.

CHAPTER 9

Explore Various Solutions

During a night shift at an assembly plant, a large fluorescent light fixture fell more than 20 feet. It suddenly smashed onto an unoccupied welding cell. Thankfully, no one was working there at the time, and no one nearby was hurt. Mark Schack, the company's engineering manager of 38 years and the supervisor of the maintenance team, had a series of questions to consider: *Why did the light fall? Was it an isolated issue? What if this happens again?*[35] He had to discover all the facts, explore various solutions, consider the consequences, and prioritize the safety of his team. Schack and his maintenance supervisor were able to make an ethical decision by following Richard Kyte's Four-Way Method for Ethical Decision Making.

As Kyte explains in his book *An Ethical Life: A Practical Guide to Ethical Reasoning*, "The Four-Way Method provides a way of participating constructively in discussions about controversial and complicated issues or cases."[36] He notes the best way to make ethical decisions is to discuss a situation in this order: truth, consequences, fairness, and character.[37] Here's a quick summary of his Four-Way Method:

TRUTH: What are the facts, relevant laws, policies, professional standards, and possible solutions? Keep any emotional or passionate opinions out of this part of the discussion.

CONSEQUENCES: Who will be affected and benefit from the possible solutions?

FAIRNESS: Do the proposed solutions treat everyone fairly and with respect and dignity?

CHARACTER: "Can the proposed solutions be enacted virtuously (i.e., compassionately, wisely, courageously, etc.)," and will the proposed solutions build trusting relationships?[38]

When Schack met with his maintenance supervisor to discuss the fallen light fixture, he initially treated it as just a fluke, an unfortunate and isolated incident. But when they started working through the Four-Way Method, especially when discussing consequences, they knew what needed to be done for the greater good. Here's a summary of their discussion:[39]

TRUTH: One light fixture fell. It was about 4 feet long by 2–3 feet wide. The light fixture had six LED fluorescent bulbs. They broke. Each fixture was held in place about 22 feet in the air. There were hundreds of light fixtures in the assembly plant. No one was hurt, but it could have been a life-threatening injury if it had landed on a welder. There were several possible solutions, including (1) treating this as an isolated incident, (2) inspecting a handful of light fixtures, and (3) inspecting all (hundreds of) light fixtures.

CONSEQUENCES: As Schack and the mainte-
nance supervisor considered each possible solution, they
discussed the consequences: (1) If they chose to treat this
as an isolated incident, there would be no further inspec-
tion. Moving on would allow the maintenance team to
work on other projects and potentially save money on re-
pairs/replacements. However, welders and other guests
in the building would not know whether it was truly an
isolated incident. Additional fixtures could fail. People
could be hurt or killed. (2) If they chose to inspect a
handful of light fixtures, it would take some project pri-
oritization and effort by the maintenance team. This solution would not ensure the safety of the entire facility.
People could be hurt or killed if a similar incident oc-
curred. (3) If they chose to inspect all (hundreds of) light
fixtures, this solution would take the entire maintenance
team away from other priorities. It could be costly if the
fixtures needed to be replaced or parts repaired. The in-
spection and possible repairs would take days. But this
appeared to be the only way to be 100% sure the situation
was either an isolated incident or systemic. This solution
would also ensure the facility was safe for everyone working under the lights or walking through the building.

Once they discussed the consequences, Schack and
his maintenance supervisor noted they had essentially
come to a conclusion. They knew they needed to inspect
all the lights. While they believed they were leaning

toward the right, ethical decision, they continued to discuss the rest of the Four-Way Method.

FAIRNESS: The maintenance team would take the brunt of the additional work and need to reprioritize projects. However, Schack and the maintenance supervisor found it was not fair or respectful to make welders risk injury under light fixtures that may fail. Other people who would walk through the building were also not safe.

CHARACTER: Reputations were on the line. If Schack and the maintenance supervisor didn't show respect for the safety and well-being of their direct reports, they would erode trust, which is difficult to regain. The company's reputation was also on the line. Not only did they have to fulfill their mission of improving people's lives with the products they manufacture and sell to the general public, but they had to keep their promise of providing a healthy and safe environment for their employees. Plus, they could have faced legal action and damaged their brand.

Ultimately, Schack noted, the maintenance team replaced the one light that had fallen. While inspecting all the other fixtures, the team discovered that the air makeup system throughout the plant would blow and cause the lights to wiggle a bit. If the S-hook were not properly installed, the fixture would become loose and could fall. Several of the fixtures were repaired. Once the project was complete, the company did not have another fixture fail.

"I always look at the trusting relationships thing," Schack said. "So often we can do such a great job in caring for others just by getting to the second or third step of the Four-Way Method. My advice would be to use it and use it often. It becomes much easier to apply if you use it frequently."

Schack keeps a laminated copy of Kyte's Four-Way Method for Ethical Decision Making in his project management folder. While some decisions need to be made rather quickly, most of the time we can incorporate Kyte's Four-Way Method to ensure the same set of reasoning, **explore various solutions**, and come to an agreement even if not everyone is happy with the decision.

Reflection Questions

1. How do you know you're making an ethical decision?
2. What does an ethical organization look like?
3. Who do you entrust in your life to have discussions about ethical situations or issues?

Action Items

1. Explain an ethical situation from a recent movie or TV show. Use Richard Kyte's Four-Way Method for Ethical Decision Making and discuss the outcome.
2. Describe a situation in which you felt an unethical decision was made and how that impacted you personally or professionally.
3. Review your organization's code of ethics or create one of your own.

CHAPTER 10

Go Glitch Hunt

A standard letter arrived in the mail. It was an automated send from the U.S. Department of Veterans Affairs (VA) in Washington, DC, about seeing a particular doctor at an outpatient clinic. The problem was that the letter was addressed to a military veteran who had died earlier that year.[40] Naturally, the veteran's family was distraught. They didn't need another reminder—no matter the age of the veteran or circumstance surrounding the death—that their loved one was gone, especially from a health care organization that no longer needed to provide patient care. Family members contacted the U.S. Congress, the governing body of the VA, and asked them to prevent the problem from happening again. Congress tasked VA leaders to identify who messed up and how to solve the issue. At first, it appeared to be a witch hunt.

About five departments were involved in the discussion. Each one blamed another. There was a lack of trust. People feared they would be fired if they spoke up. They circled the wagon. Linda W. Belton, a senior executive in the Veterans Health Administration, advised her direct report to sit down with the group and work to identify the basics of what people agreed on. She did so and found they all agreed they had a commitment to veterans and their families.

"Then they could start talking about, 'What does that mean in this particular case?'" Belton said. "And so the finger-pointing stopped, and they were able to come up with an absolutely marvelous systems redesign. But it took a lot of trust."

The team was able to move from a witch hunt to a glitch hunt.[41] It's easy to point fingers and place blame. It's much more difficult and important to take a step back and engage in system fixes, not scapegoating. Belton spent 10 years running the Wisconsin state hospital system and 20 years as a senior executive running a system of VA hospitals for the federal government. Before retiring, she switched from running hospitals to being a director of organizational health for the last 8 years. That's where she worked to spread the word about the importance of servant leadership, which has been adopted by the VA as its leadership model.

Belton notes glitch hunts happen in two ways: retrospectively and prospectively. In the preceding case, and at most organizations, glitch hunts happen retrospectively after a mistake, problem, or crisis occurs. Prospectively, the VA created a systems improvement department, participated in a "deep dive" twice a year to identify and solve more immediate problems, and created rapid improvement teams.

"The best fixes come from the people who work with those systems every day and the customers who use those systems," Belton said.

For example, nurses at a VA hospital in Indianapolis teamed up to figure out how to be more economical in steps to provide better care for their coworkers and patients. They made a diagram of a particular nursing unit and drew lines where nurses went during the day. They compiled their data and proposed reconfiguring the nursing unit so that people's steps were minimized. It was approved.

"Glitch hunts versus witch hunts is about moral authority," Belton said. "To get to the moral authority, we've got to inspire trust. And I think that's essential to solving problems and preventing problems."

Belton further explained servant leaders simplify processes so there are fewer chances to make mistakes, errors, or glitches. They foster the systems thinking, or systems redesign, process.

"They don't own that process," Belton said. "They're a steward of that process. They want everybody to understand and contribute to the process as well."

It's important to see how things connect. When something goes wrong, leaders should identify parts of the system that need to be redesigned so the same issue does not happen again instead of blaming someone as the problem. **Go glitch hunt.**

Reflection Questions

1. Describe a situation in which you witnessed a witch hunt. How would the situation have been different if it was a glitch hunt instead?

2. How are people able to submit feedback for improvement at your organization?

3. How have you or someone you know redesigned a system to solve a problem?

Action Items

1. Create a systems improvement team.

2. Review issues that have been resolved at home or work. Identify patterns to see if the problems are similar and if a systems redesign could be necessary.

3. Talk to a mentor about an issue they experienced and discuss how they came to a solution.

CHAPTER 11

We Experience Lifequakes

My husband and I were leisurely watching the live broadcast of *Monday Night Football* on January 2, 2023. The Cincinnati Bengals were leading the Buffalo Bills 7–3 with about six minutes left in the first quarter. Bills safety Damar Hamlin made a common tackle after a pass completion. But when he stood up, he suddenly fell backwards. Hamlin was resuscitated on the field and taken to a hospital in critical condition. Play did not resume. We were worried and joined the players of both teams in praying for Hamlin's recovery. As we later learned, the direct blow to Hamlin's chest at *just* the right time in his heart rhythm caused cardiac arrest due to commotio cordis, a rare condition.[42] Thanks to quick actions by trained medical professionals at the game and additional care he received, the 24-year-old was able to begin his recovery at the hospital and reflect on his larger purpose in life. What Hamlin experienced—and what millions of people saw live—is what author Bruce Feiler calls a "lifequake," or an incredibly disruptive experience that alters your life in a significant way.

"Lifequakes are massive, messy, and often miserable," Feiler wrote in his book *Life Is in the Transitions: Mastering Change at Any Age*. "They come at inconvenient times that usually make them more inconvenient.

They aggregate. But they also do something else: They initiate a period of self-reflection and personal reevaluation. They set in motion a series of reverberations that lead us to revisit our own identity."[43]

As Feiler notes, we experience an average of three-to-five lifequakes in a lifetime.[44] They may come, in addition to a medical episode, in the form of the death of a loved one, a financial crisis, or a divorce. Hamlin had to take care of his physical and mental health in order to make a comeback once cleared by medical professionals. He was able to return to practice in April. During his first news conference, he thanked everyone who had medically cared for him and wished him well. He expressed his courage and confidence to continue his pro football career. He played in the preseason in August and was back in a regular-season game in October, which the Bills won.

"It felt amazing," Hamlin said at a news conference after that game. "You know, the energy from the fans was amazing. Just being able to be out there with my teammates. I had my family in the stands. Everybody on the team gives me confidence, just feeds me positive energy, positive everything all week long. To just get out there and play with everybody again just felt amazing."[45]

Through this experience, Hamlin also found a larger purpose. He raised awareness of the rare cardiac condition commotio cordis and emphasized the importance of cardiopulmonary resuscitation (CPR) and automated external defibrillators (AEDs), especially during youth athletic events. As part of his Chasing M's Foundation, Hamlin partnered with the American Heart Association to create a CPR Tour. It launched in summer 2023 in Pittsburgh, where he played college football.

"Because of what happened to me, I'm working to make sure that kids across the country have the same access to life-saving care that I did if they need it," Hamlin said.[46]

I followed Hamlin's journey closely that year. I had hoped he would make a full recovery. I was inspired by his desire to continue moving forward, by his understanding about when he knew he was ready to return, and by his determination to help improve others' lives because of what he learned from his traumatic experience. Unless you're in the public eye as a sports personality or celebrity, most lifequakes aren't as public as Hamlin's. From my experience with lifequakes, such as losing a loved one, they tend to impact every part of your life, and the overall experience may be similar to dealing with grief. You may question your faith or lean on it more, you may choose a different career path or dig deeper into your daily work, and you may struggle in various ways or find new tools to help you move forward.

Feiler discovered seven tools as part of a "transition tool kit" that can help us navigate lifequakes: "Accept it (Identify your emotions), Mark it (Ritualize the change),

Shed it (Give up old mind-sets), Create it (Try new things), Share it (Seek wisdom from others), Launch it (Unveil your new self), and Tell it (Compose a fresh story)."[47] While we may not need all of these tools at once, it is a good idea to note them and identify what we need to focus on the most at the time. We need to find the right support system, give ourselves grace to work through emotional and physical challenges, and find ways to persevere. As servant leaders, we need to find ways to navigate personal lifequakes and also help team-mates at work find the support they need to move for-ward. What impacts our personal life impacts our pro-fessional life, and vice versa. When **we experience lifequakes**, our focus shifts, we learn to adapt to our "new normal," and we look for deeper meaning. It's hard to say why lifequakes happen, but when they do, we need to realize that a setback may be a redirect in disguise. Or we just need time to hope and heal.

Reflection Questions
1. Who is in your support system to help you navigate impactful life events?
2. How did you overcome or work through a lifequake?
3. What resources do you need when a disruptive event happens in your life?

Action Items
1. Write a journal entry about one lifequake that either you've experienced or your family has experienced. Provide details about the situation, how life changed after it, and what you learned.
2. Research a lifequake that affected a community in a different country (i.e., a natural disaster or an impactful news story). How did they work through or overcome the situation?
3. Ask your supervisor or human resources department about ways your organization can help you work through a lifequake.

CHAPTER 12

We Share Hope

Twelve-year-old Ayan was excited for her family vacation. She wore her favorite dress. It was yellow with pink flowers. Ayan brought some of her stuffed animals and photos along for the trip. As her family finished packing, Ayan suddenly realized they were in trouble. Their vacation was actually an evacuation. Ayan and her family had to leave their home in Mogadishu, Somalia. They were no longer safe. They had to flee as refugees.[48]

Ayan had to rapidly change her clothes. She was told that as a young girl, wearing a dress made her more vulnerable to assault. Ayan and her extended family could only bring what they could carry. In the coming days, they walked hundreds and hundreds of miles. As they continued, they had to leave things behind. Initially, they left photo albums and clothes. At one point, they had to make a choice between carrying water and carrying food. That was followed by an even more excruciating decision. They had to leave people behind. Members of Ayan's family and other companions could no longer walk. Some were not strong enough to stand on their own. Ayan had to leave her cousin behind. Somehow, she found the strength to keep moving forward.

Ayan shared her story with Chicago-based documentary artist James A. Bowey. He began his career as a war photographer and now writes and exhibits on the complexities, challenges, and possibilities of human connection. As part of his interview process, Bowey actively listened to Ayan's traumatic story. He listens for what he considers "found poems." He describes these as distilled moments in a person's story that reveal the depths of being human in a challenging world. His work combines visual art and personal stories to create a dialogue with the audience.

Ayan's story is part of Bowey's traveling exhibition, *When Home Won't Let You Stay: Stories of Refugees in America*.

Ayan, 2016[49]
Home: Mogadishu, Somalia

I was 12 years old.
I wore my best dress, like we were taking a trip.
But fleeing means you let go of everything you can't carry.
First it was the photographs and clothes,
then the food, and water.
You get to the point where you can only carry yourself,
and death would be better.
Somehow you continue.

Bowey has covered dozens of stories from people "on the razor's edge of life" and has worked on a variety of subject matters. While everyone's journey is different, a dominant theme emerges: hope.

"Hope is not the end point," Bowey explains. "Hope is the middle ground between an impossible present and a possible future."[50]

From his experience, very rarely do people use the word *hope* while they're going through trauma or a profound experience; it's usually used in retrospect or by listeners or analysts trying to better understand someone else's situation and imagine how they were able to carry on.

"Hope is a profound acceptance," Bowey continues. "Hope means things change in often unpredictable ways, and so does our capacity to adapt. We will discover a new center within ourselves, new connections to others, and new understanding that we could not have imagined before. We may not get the outcome we desire; what we get is transformation."

At a young age, Ayan had to accept the alarming reality that she had to leave her home and sense of security forever.

"You get to the point where you can only carry yourself, and death would be better," Ayan said. "Somehow you continue."

While she didn't use the word *hope*, she definitely described it. She faced an abrupt change to her life and found the will to move forward. She hoped she would be strong enough. She hoped she would find safety. She hoped for a better life.

Ayan is now a wife, mother, and businessperson living in Minnesota. Her story gives hope to others. That is ultimately hope's lasting power.

"**We share hope**," Bowey advises. "If a person near me feels less hope, so too do I. If a person near me feels more hope, so too do I. Our own hope is connected to the hope of others. Hope is what connects us all."

Reflection Questions
1. How do you define hope?
2. What gives you hope?
3. In what ways do you share hope?

Action Items
1. Describe a situation in which you struggled with initial acceptance or felt hopeless at the time and how, in retrospect, hope helped you move forward.
2. Research a story in which someone did not have food, water, shelter, or safety—our most basic human needs. Identify their struggles and explain how they describe hope.
3. Identify an organization that helps people in your community. Decide whether to donate your time, talent, or treasure. Then reflect on how you share hope through your decision.

CHAPTER 13

On Your Heart

During my stream-of-consciousness storytelling session, my spiritual director would nod, smile, and gently encourage me to continue processing everything on my mind. I had a lot to say about work projects, family gatherings, tidying the house, and trying to stay warm during winter in Wisconsin. I talked about "snowbirds," retirees who would fly to Florida for the season, and recent concerns about iguanas. If the temperature dropped into the 40s Fahrenheit, iguanas might become immobile and fall from trees because they're cold-blooded. They are usually just stunned when they fall, the National Weather Service Miami–South Florida reassured me, and make a full recovery.[51]

Apparently, no one had brought up iguanas falling from trees in the four years Sister Sarah Hennessey had been a spiritual director at the Franciscan Spirituality Center.[52] She was surprised by my visual description and laughed, which made me laugh. I was appreciative that Sister Sarah just let my mind wander, but when I paused long enough in conversation, she asked me a particular question that made me slow down and think differently.

"What's **on your heart**?"

Oh, that's deep.

That question is at the core of spiritual direction, which is nonjudgmental, compassionate, deep listening.

"It's important to drop down, drop out of the head," Sister Sarah said. "Drop into feelings, emotions. That's where so much of our wisdom lies. I think also sometimes it's important to drop into the body as well."[53]

Counseling is more about problem solving, advice giving, and teaching. Sister Sarah notes that spiritual direction is recognizing, "I have the wisdom within me as the speaker and touching into that wisdom. And there's also a sense where there is something mysterious."

During spiritual direction sessions, Sister Sarah listens to people with different backgrounds and beliefs, ranging from agnostics to those who are very orthodox in their faith. Some use language ranging from God to Divine Mystery. After learning the language they use for the holy, she asks questions such as the following: *What brings you here? What would you like out of our time together? What are you desiring?*

Work and relationships are the top two topics people address in the 45–55-minute sessions. People also tend to talk about spiritual issues, trauma, or some sort of suffering. There is a power in being heard, in someone listening to your story even if you're not sure what you're going to say. Sister Sarah said:

I remember going to one of my own spiritual direction sessions, and I started out thinking I don't know what I'm going to talk about today. There's not much going on. We had a little bit of silence and she asked, "Well, what's on your heart?" and I just started weeping. And then I was like, "I don't know if I'm supposed to be here anymore." You know, these huge existential questions about my life and meaning and call and purpose and all of these questions I didn't even think were there. And she just created a little bit of space, and then it all poured out.

She said that session was a huge turning point for working through her depression. Her spiritual director actively listened and acknowledged her struggle.

Depending on the situation, spiritual directors will refer individuals to counseling where they can receive additional assistance. Attending counseling or spiritual direction sessions is about giving yourself grace to work through difficult life situations that arise. Some may find spiritual direction is not for them, and they move on after one session. Some people may need one or two more sessions to sort out their feelings. Others continue to return for several sessions each year.

When I notice my thoughts seem to pile up and start to weigh me down, that's when I need someone outside of my immediate family and close friends to listen and help me to get out of my head and focus on what's on my heart. We need spiritual directors and counselors to help guide us and deeply listen as we sort through situations.

Just remember to draw the focus back to what's **on your heart**.

Reflection Questions
1. How do you listen to what's on your heart?
2. How do you sort through your thoughts and ideas?
3. How do you know you are well?

Action Items
1. Identify who you can share what's on your heart with.
2. Explore your organization's options for spiritual direction or counseling, such as an employee assistance program.
3. Identify a time in your life when you've been deeply listened to and how that impacted you.

CHAPTER 14

Humor Can Heal

I stood by my vehicle's trunk and made a few adjustments. I had to make sure the dinosaur was comfortable in the tote bag. Its head and legs were dangling dramatically. *That should be noticeable*, I thought. I was asked to bring the dinosaur to the café so my new friend would recognize me. A hostess asked if I needed help. I mentioned I was meeting someone and looked to my left. That's when I saw a lady staring at me holding a bullhorn and fake cigarette at a nearby table. *That must be Lisa*, I thought.

Lisa David Olson is a business humorist, author, and interactive speaker who has been performing in front of audiences for more than 20 years. She has been part of Heart of La Crosse, a comedy troupe known for sketches, musical parodies, and improvisation—her favorite. When Lisa responded to my initial email request for an interview, we agreed on a time, date, and location.

"How will we know each other?" Lisa asked. "Do you, by chance, have one of those inflatable T. rex costumes?"

Surprisingly, I did not. I was able to borrow one from a friend for the occasion, but it seemed rather delicate, so I decided not to wear it. The morning of our meeting, Lisa emailed her distinguishable items.

Early on in our coffee conversation, Lisa explained the influence comedian and actress Carol Burnett had on her life.[54]

"I pretended she was my mom, and she'd help me get through stuff," Lisa said. "She also grew up in an alcoholic home."[55]

When her mother would drink alcohol, she would physically abuse Lisa and her three siblings. They used humor to try to cheer each other up. Laughter and applause helped fill a void. They also noticed that humor would sometimes change their mother's mood and she wouldn't be as violent. However, there was a moment when the pain felt like it was too much and Lisa thought about ending her life. She was staring at a handful of pills when she heard the comedian laugh. *The Carol Burnett Show* was on the TV in the other room.

"Her laughter stopped me," Lisa said. "I chose laughter in that moment. Life is about choices. I chose laughter, humor."[56]

Laughter has many benefits, including increasing the endorphins released by the brain, soothing tensions, and improving your immune system.[57] It can also help relieve pain.

"We are drawn to humor," Lisa said.

She paused.

I looked up from taking notes.

Her attention was focused on four young men who had entered the café. Three of them were wearing twin-size mattresses.

"You should take a serious selfie with them," I said. But before I got halfway through the sentence, she was gone.

"Guys, can I get a picture?" she asked, two tables away. They happily agreed. Lisa and I had earlier discussed how she loves taking selfies with strangers, and this was a perfect moment.[58]

"No smiles," she informed them.

"Game face," one of them replied.

All but mattress number one complied. He just couldn't keep that big grin off his face!

"I'm really in the market for a pillow," Lisa told them.

"We got pillows, comforters, everything," said mattress number one, clearly the head salesman.

"And if you buy a mattress, get a free comforter," mattress number two said.

"And sheets," mattress number three added.

"You sleep a third of your life away," the spokesman with a sign said.

"Want to announce?" Lisa asked, handing them her megaphone.

"Oh, can we use this? Will they be mad?"

"Yeah, they will, but life is short," Lisa replied.

"Just start your message in the back of the café," I chimed in. "They'll kick you out, but you'll get your message across first."

They chose to not take our ill-advised (but would-be-successful) marketing ideas.

Laughter was contagious at this point.

We learned they were selling mattresses a couple of blocks away for a local high school football fundraiser. We were talking with the quarterback, running back, and wide receivers. The conversation continued at our table.

"What kind of mattress are you wearing?" I asked.

"This is generic."

"This is a Sleep Number," mattress number one said.

"What's your number, man?" Lisa asked.

He said his phone number out loud.

We laughed harder.

"Is it free delivery?" I asked.

"YES! To your OWN home!"

"You'll deliver to Indiana?"[59]

"Yes, anywhere!"

"We'll even get your old mattress out."

"When is this sale?" I asked and then read the sign. "It's from 10 to 4:30? It's 10:30! You're losing customers."

"We needed an ice-cold beverage."

"Stay hydrated but don't wet the mattress," I said as they started for the door.

"Stains are not good," Lisa confirmed.

They walked out smiling and laughing with cups of water in their hands.

"I feel very pleased that happened," I said, smiling at Lisa.

"Me too."

We shared a short laughter duet.

"I love that he was a Sleep Number and he gave me *his* number!" Lisa said. "Maybe if I still needed a babysitter or someone to mow my lawn I would call."

It was a brilliant, ridiculous five-minute improvisation session. We said "Yes, and" quite a lot, which is the basic rule of improv. *Yes, that's a thing, and how about this?* You support your castmates and build off of each other to ensure success.

"Humor is so important," Lisa said. "But you can't just always be on. Not everything is funny at a hospital, a police station, in a family situation. But knowing when to have levity is really important."

Laughter can lighten a mood. Humor can build connection and bring people together, which is Lisa's goal as a speaker and workshop leader. Later in life, Lisa and her mother were able to discuss some of the traumatic things from her childhood. Her mother, who was able to get sober, spoke of her regret and the pain she caused her children from self-medicating a mental illness they never talked about growing up. Her mother also encouraged Lisa to perform—even before they made amends—and use humor to help others. **Humor can heal.**

"Humor is my escape," Lisa said. "Writing is my creative outlet. Performing is my joy."

Reflection Questions
1. In what ways can you bring a little levity to work?
2. What comedians make you laugh? Why?
3. How do you rediscover joy after a tragedy?

Action Items
1. Tell a story about something you found amusing lately.
2. Buy a calendar you find hilarious.
3. Note local comedy troupes, comedians, and upcoming events that you could consider attending.

Repurpose Your Tools

In her book, *F.I.E.R.C.E.: Transform Your Life in the Face of Adversity, 5 Minutes at a Time!*[60] Carolyn Colleen explains how she survived abusive situations as a child and as an adult and how she worked her way out of poverty as a single mom while going to college. She later earned a master of business administration and PhD in organizational leadership. After years of working diligently for others, she became an entrepreneur and speaker, sharing her story to help others with *heartfelt intensity*.[61] Through profound introspection of her past adversities and processing past trauma, Carolyn discovered a powerful formula for personal and community transformation.

"In life, we are either in a storm, coming out of a storm, or heading right into one," Carolyn said. "Life doesn't necessarily get easier. We just learn to navigate better."[62]

To work through her adversities, Carolyn went to therapy, identified mentors, and surrounded herself with people who believed in her and reminded her to build on her strengths. As she reflected on pivotal moments in her life, Carolyn realized the adversity might be different, but the tools used to overcome a challenge in the past can be repurposed and reused for the current challenge. She realized a profound truth—"success leaves clues"—and created her F.I.E.R.C.E. 5 Method:

Focused breath: take a deep breath, face fear, and focus.

Identify one goal; name three things required to achieve that goal.

Examine barriers to the goal.

Reflect and visualize your truths; co-create your own reality.

Courage: recognize that you have the courage.

Engage—take action![63]

Her tools, once repurposed, soon became the building blocks for a 20-year goal: a nonprofit organization dedicated to transformation through education, access, and community. The FIERCE Foundation helps underserved women create generational self-sufficiency in La Crosse, Wisconsin, and beyond. When women begin the program, they receive mental well-being support in the form of therapy and a behavior coach.

"FIERCE navigators, which are mentors, give women permission to dream first, give hope, and then navigate those dreams and hope through programming," Carolyn said.

As they progress through the program, participants may be referred to other nonprofits in the community to help them reach their individual goals. For example, if a person within a lower income bracket wants to own a home, they may be referred to connect with Couleecap to work on a budget and identify financial assistance programs for first-time homeowners. If they want to be the best parent they can be, they may connect with the Family and Children's Center to enroll in programs to cope with the stress and demands of raising children.

"We're elevating off of systems," Carolyn said. "We're the door, not the doer. I strongly feel that we need to be able to collaborate more as humans and compete less in order for our world to continue to thrive."

By using her experience overcoming adversities, she is setting other people on the path to success. That's the difficult and life-changing work of a servant leader. In his book *Servant Leadership: A Journey into the Nature of Legitimate Power and Greatness*, Robert Greenleaf wrote:

> The best test, and difficult to administer, is this: Do those served grow as persons? Do they, *while being served*, become healthier, wiser, freer, more autonomous, more likely themselves to become servants? *And*, what is the effect on the least privileged in society? Will they benefit or at least not be further deprived?[64]

Once women progress through the FIERCE Foundation's program, they have the opportunity to give back to a new woman entering the program and donate time, talent, or treasure back—just like Carolyn has done for her community.

"As you come out on the other side, you've learned to **repurpose your tools**," Carolyn said. "Use the tools you already have. Build up that grit. Build up that resilience. And then evolve into your new definition of self."

Carolyn is working to collect data from the FIERCE Foundation to show how to reverse the effects of adverse childhood experiences, address disparities, and create a healing community. She's also contributing to the conversation as a delegate at the United Nations Commission on the Status of Women, which was established in 1946 to promote gender equality and the empowerment of women.[65] Each year, women from around the world meet in New York City to discuss recommendations to the United Nations General Assembly and collaborate to draw more attention to and make improvements to women's equality and well-being.

"Being in the UN itself was a long-term goal," Carolyn said. "It was really the aligning of all the different occurrences in my life that got me into the space that I'm in now. The developing of relationships and the development of self. To believe, to understand that I deserve to be in that room with the work that I've put in."

The work she's put in is difficult and daring and improves not only her life, but the lives of the people she serves as an entrepreneur and community leader. When you repurpose your tools, you'll find ways to overcome adversities and be able to assist other people in your life and community.

Reflection Questions
1. What tools have you used to overcome an adversity in your life?
2. Reflect on a past or current adversity. What new meaning can you give to this experience?
3. Who helps you navigate through difficult challenges or helps navigate your personal and professional goals?

Action Items
1. Interview a family member, friend, or colleague about how they overcame a challenge in their life and how they were able to overcome it. Identify themes and see if you can incorporate them into your life or as a mentor.
2. Explore ways to get involved in a national conversation you're passionate about that can improve people's lives.
3. Identify individuals who can be part of your personal advisory team, including areas such as finances, career goals, or family support.

CHAPTER 16

Rethink the Situation

When she was 14 years old, Natalie Jankowski was diagnosed with adolescent idiopathic scoliosis, a sideways curvature of the spine that has no definite cause. Anything above a 10-degree curvature is diagnosable as scoliosis. Natalie's thoracic spine, or the middle of her back, had a 52-degree curve.[66] That's considered very severe. Her back was shaped like the letter *S*. There is no cure for scoliosis, but surgery helps straighten the spine to alleviate pain and other impacts on the body later in life. Three days after completing her first high school basketball season, Natalie had major surgery.

In early February 2001, two permanent stainless steel rods were placed on either side of her spine.[67] Technically, she had a spinal fusion, as bone was scraped from her hips to fuse together with the rods. Her curvature is now down to 26 degrees, which is still considered moderate scoliosis. After surgery, she was in the hospital for six days and was walking again on day three. She was out of school for a few months, and a tutor helped her at home. When she returned, she had half days and couldn't carry weight on her back, so she had to carry everything in her hands, including all of her books for class.

"It was a whole thing, but it worked out," Natalie said, maintaining a positive mindset.

While Natalie had some limitations after surgery and proceeded with caution, she had to test how her body would react. About 10 months after surgery, Natalie played her first varsity basketball game. But she stayed away from playing forward because she didn't initially like the idea of defenders placing their hand on her back so soon. In track, she was no longer able to do the high jump.

"That was an automatic, 'Nope, can't do that anymore.' But I can't jump very high as it is, so I was like, 'Not a problem,'" Natalie said with a laugh.

She was advised to rethink riding roller coasters in which your feet dangle. Since "it wasn't a hard no," she tested that theory by going on Batman: The Ride, her favorite at Six Flags Great America in Gurnee, Illinois. Unfortunately, the harness and seat put pressure on her spine, and she almost passed out. She decided to ride one more time.

"A lot of my experiences have been I'm not going to know how my body reacts until I do it, and now I know not to go on Batman," Natalie said, laughing. She has also ruled out zip lines and bungee jumping (prior to the experience).

How do you know? That's a question Natalie frequently asks to better understand her abilities, a situation, or a possible outcome. There is value in rethinking by using that phrase. In his book *Think Again*, Adam Grant states we should ask that question more often.

"The power lies in its frankness," Grant wrote. "It's nonjudgmental—a straightforward expression of doubt and curiosity that doesn't put people on the defensive."[68]

About 13 years after her surgery, Natalie's shoulders were causing her discomfort. She noticed they were rounded forward. She sought the assistance of a physical therapist who had experience with scoliosis. That's when she started strength training, another thing she wasn't sure how her back would react to until she started doing it. Exercises such as a lateral pull-down and a dumbbell row with 3–8-lb. weights relieved her pain and helped improve her posture.[69]

"There's a fine line between doing too much, not doing enough, and doing just enough," Natalie said. "The maintenance level is where I'm at for a lot of it."

In high school, Natalie ran the 800 m and the 3,200 m relay. She preferred shorter distances and ran several 5Ks (3.1 mi.) and 10Ks (6.2 mi.) until her husband recommended they train for a half marathon (13.1 mi.) at Walt Disney World, where she had worked as a character performer as part of the Disney College Program and later as a part-time employee. Natalie typically uses the Run Walk Run method made famous by Olympian Jeff Galloway.[70] It helps her catch her breath, lowers her blood pressure, and reduces a bit of pounding on the pavement. Thankfully, her training paid off, and she completed the half marathon with minimal back discomfort, so they set their sights on the 2018 New York City Marathon (26.2 mi.). Natalie had to mentally and physically figure out how she was going to tack on the extra mileage, fuel properly, and work in strength training.

"We did one 20-mile training run, and it's like, alright, we're in the great unknown," Natalie thought as they started mile 21 during the race. "I literally didn't know what was going to happen. I was feeling a little trepidation."

But she kept moving forward with a positive mindset. Natalie felt a huge sense of accomplishment when they crossed that finish line. Surprisingly, her back did not hurt. She had proved she could accomplish her goal. Yet, she is not planning on signing up for an ultramarathon anytime soon.

Grant notes, "As we question our current understanding, we become curious about what information we're missing. The search leads us to new discoveries, which in turn maintain our humility by reinforcing how much we still have to learn. If knowledge is power, knowing what we don't know is wisdom."[71]

When she was younger, Natalie didn't know anyone with scoliosis. Now she is part of a larger community on social media where she can share her scoliosis story and connect with others. She has learned that every body is different. She's happy to see advancements in medical technology for the next generation, such as 3D-printed back braces that try to slow down the scoliosis curve progression. The braces are now more form-fitted to the individual patient, colorful, and decorative. Natalie wore her "hideous," thick plastic, Velcro-strapped back brace under clothes in eighth grade—something she never wanted anyone to see. But she's never been afraid to show her scar after surgery. She was especially fond of her open-back wedding dress, which put her scar on display as she walked down the aisle. While her diagnosis and surgery limited a few activities, it provided her with an opportunity to **rethink the situation** and be more introspective. Natalie found different ways to care for her body, accomplish new goals with the support of her in-person and online community, and realize she is "scoliosis strong."

Reflection Questions

1. What do you think are some of your limiting beliefs?
2. What is a current situation you need to rethink?
3. What is something you didn't think you could do but now realize you are more than capable of doing?

Action Items

1. Start to incorporate the question, *How do you know?* into your life, especially when you need to rethink a situation.
2. Identify ways in which you can improve a situation with a more positive mindset.
3. Meet with diversity, equity, and inclusion teams at your organization or in your community to identify opportunities to rethink situations that could be improved for people with physical limitations or disabilities.

CHAPTER 17

Take a Walk

Every morning, Stephanie Ross takes her energetic Siberian husky named Yuka for a walk. Their original intent was to just establish a routine and get some fresh air and exercise, especially on a crisp winter morning. What they've discovered is that their daily walk is a way to create stronger connections with their neighbors, stay grounded in nature, and allow for creative problem-solving breakthroughs (at least for Stephanie).

Occasionally, Stephanie will listen to a podcast while she's walking. However, most of the time, she's just present in the moment and listening to natural sound.

"I'm always asking for signs during walks, and my sign has always been a feather," Stephanie said. "I always see one. It's funny because sometimes it'll be the tiniest little feather, and other times it's massive like an eagle feather."[72]

While she's looking for a sign, Stephanie lets her mind wander. She's come home from walks with creative solutions to problems, ideas to incorporate into her business ventures, and reasons she should make a purposeful pivot. When she was 20 years old and going to college, Stephanie launched her first business, a lifestyle wellness community for women. Ten years later, she shifted its focus after redefining success, reevaluating her goals, and finding her sense of fulfillment. She now coaches small business owners through her company, Small Business Sister Circle, and she is a realtor.

"I need to go for a walk and just see what comes," Stephanie said. "You're going to get clarity, and at least you're going to get some peace and quiet, which is what you need for your higher self and your intuition to come through. I think peace and quiet is what a lot of our society is lacking."

In her book *Bored and Brilliant: How Spacing Out Can Unlock Your Most Productive and Creative Self*, Manoush Zomorodi emphasizes the importance of letting our minds wander and allowing them to be naturally creative and solve problems.[73]

"When our minds wander, we activate something called the 'default mode,' the mental place where we solve problems and generate our best ideas, and engage in what's known as 'autobiographical planning,' which is how we make sense of our world and our lives and set future goals. The default mode is also involved in how we try to understand and empathize with other people, and make moral judgments."[74]

Stephanie wants to provide opportunities for people in her community to let their minds wander when they go for a walk so they can see the benefits she's experienced. She has led small groups on a hike and meditate event.

"We usually get to the peak and do a meditation," Stephanie said, referring to a hike atop a bluff. "I'll bring focus to an anchor in the present moment—the ground, leaves, insects, wind—techniques I've learned through my training in yoga and mindfulness. Usually we start with gratitude."

In his book *The Nature Principle: Reconnecting with Life in a Virtual Age*, Richard Louv notes, there is "a growing body of theoretical, anecdotal, and empirical research that describes the restorative power of nature— its impact on our senses and intelligence; on our physical, psychological, and spiritual health; and on the bonds of family, friendship, and the multi-species community."[75]

When you **take a walk**, you can also step away from a stressful or tense situation, regroup after working for hours on a project, or disconnect a bit from your dependence on technology. Stephanie has noticed that her hiking group enjoys being on a trail and taking in the view. They've thanked her for guiding them on a trail that they can now enjoy with their families and have a sense of adventure close to home. Thankfully, Stephanie has a daily reminder to let her mind wander each morning when Yuka goes to the front door and requests they go for a walk.

Reflection Questions

1. When was the last time you went on a walk? What did you think about?
2. What benefits have you discovered from being on a hiking trail or noticing things in the natural world?
3. How do you feel when you are walking or after you've returned?

Action Items

1. Build a walk break into your daily routine.
2. Discover a community organization that encourages trail hiking or running.
3. Call a friend or family member and ask if they want to go for a walk.

CHAPTER 18

Find More Awe

The first time Ethan Reed saw a kid playing with a toy based on a character he helped develop, he was in awe. It was in a Tokyo hotel hallway, and the young boy was playing with a small tiger cub plush. With large expressive eyes and a welcoming smile, the tiger wore a red turban with a jewel on top of his head between his ears.

Chandu is a beloved character from Sinbad's Storybook Voyage at Tokyo DisneySea, an attraction Reed worked on for Walt Disney Imagineering (WDI). Chandu was the first original Disney character he designed with a team.[76] He was reminded that his creative design and direction are important because they bring joy and happiness to people around the world.

Reed worked for WDI for more than 20 years. He held a wide variety of roles, including animator, art director, creative director, production designer, and visual effects supervisor. He worked on dozens of Disney Parks attractions in the United States and overseas. Reed was initially brought on as an animator for the Hong Kong Disneyland exclusive attraction Mystic Manor, which could be considered a distant cousin of the Haunted Mansion but with a completely different storyline. When the attraction was resurrected after spending nine months on the shelf, Reed was asked to work on the character designs. He made a suggestion that transformed the storyline featuring Lord Henry Mystic, a bumbling fool, and Albert, a mischievous monkey.

"I said, 'Look, guys, why don't you let me storyboard this entire attraction like a film? Loose story drawings that are not precious, but this is what Marc Davis and Al Bertino and the original Imagineers did on their attractions,'" Reed said, successfully persuading the attraction's creative director.

By pinning up the storyboards, they were able to more clearly notice holes they needed to fill, including finalizing the creative effects for the story's climax and adding impactful music. Reed was in awe that they were able to collaborate with composer Danny Elfman. His music helped people have certain emotions as they journeyed through the attraction. During cast member previews, Reed and his project manager joined the queue to observe people's reactions. They followed three young men who were initially more focused on their phones than on the detailed designs.

When they got to the preshow, Albert said, "Ni hao," or "Hello" in Chinese. That caught their attention. When they got on the ride vehicle, Reed and the project manager sat in the back. In the first room, Lord Mystic welcomes guests to the Mystic Manor and cautions Albert to stay away from the magic music box. Of course, Albert's curiosity gets the best of him. When he opens the box, magic dust starts to fill the room and flow throughout the Manor. Initially, musical instruments start to play on their own. As guests travel through the Manor, the music shifts, and more inherently dangerous things, like armor and arrows, come to life. The ride builds to a crescendo, and the last room dramatically rips apart.

"We kept looking at each other, and we're smiling because every single gag is hitting," Reed enthusiastically explained. "And then we got to the Chinese Salon where the monkey king is doing his thing. The cast members are just looking around. When the wall broke, the three of them ducked down. They were *freaked out*. They were like, 'Ahhhhh!' It was so incredible to get that reaction."

Reed and his project manager were witnessing the expression of awe, something that is beneficial for everyone. As Dacher Keltner notes in his book *Awe: The New Science of Everyday Wonder and How It Can Transform Your Life*, experiencing moments of awe can help lower our stress level and provides several positive benefits: "Being moved by awe triggers the release of oxytocin and dopamine, a calming of stress-related physiology, and vagus nerve response, systems of millions of cells working to enable us to connect, be open, and explore."[77]

It's become an explorative game for Disney fans to search for Hidden Mickeys, or a subtle representation of Mickey Mouse in the form of three small circles, on attractions. As part of his design research for Mystic Manor, Reed studied historic samurai armor on display at the Tokyo National Museum. He noticed a pattern that looked like small mouse ears in the stitching. He directed attraction sculptors to make them all Hidden Mickeys.

"So that samurai in Mystic Manor has, I believe, 78 Hidden Mickeys on it," Reed said. "There are more Hidden Mickeys on that attraction than any other attraction on the planet mainly because of that character."

Reed has made a career of visual awe by creating memorable characters, integrating visual effects to create immersive experiences, and designing toys. His profession provides a unique opportunity to create moments of awe, experience them, and be inspired by them. Keltner notes that visual design is one of the eight wonders in life in which we can find awe. The others include moral beauty, collective effervescence, nature, music, spirituality and religion, life and death, and epiphany.[78] Everyday moments of awe may come from appreciating a colorful sunset, collective laughter, a favorite plush animal, or noticing a particular detail in a work of art. When we allow ourselves to be delighted by moments of awe, we are more open to childlike wonder that can inspire us and help us experience the vast mysteries of life. We need to **find more awe**.

Reflection Questions
1. What is your favorite theme park attraction?
2. Which of the eight wonders in life inspire you?
3. How can you find more awe in everyday life?

Action Items
1. List things that bring you joy.
2. Write how you feel when you experience a moment of awe.
3. Draw something—a figment of your imagination—and explain your creative process.

CHAPTER 19

Observations Identify Opportunity

Michael and Bryan were walking down a hallway on the first floor of an abandoned asylum when they heard a loud fan. They discovered the sound was coming from a struggling old desktop computer left in a large room. Bryan initially pushed a button to turn off the computer. When he turned the computer back on, it rebooted with a login and password screen. He clicked cancel, which instantly brought them to the desktop where they could open a handful of files. They found confidential patient names and procedure information. They blurred out confidential info in their YouTube video, which, as of this writing, has more than 3 million views.[79]

The Proper People created their urban exploration YouTube channel with the goal of traveling to abandoned manmade structures across the United States and around the world and sharing their unique video footage in a documentary style.[80] Besides walking on land and in buildings, Michael and Bryan do not disrupt the natural decay, they do not vandalize, and they do not take anything with them when they leave.[81] They tend to keep their exact location hidden and usually wait to publish their videos until a new development unfolds (demolition, remodel, increased security, etc.) that decreases the likelihood of others finding the location, getting the same footage, and causing unnecessary vandalism.

While their work is not an environmental steward-ship project in the traditional sense, their videos reveal natural decay and what happens when humans leave buildings unattended, allow them to fall into disrepair, and give nature time to partially reinherit the land. The Proper People have been to abandoned schools, hospitals, amusement parks, hotels, theaters, prisons, malls, power plants, mansions, and other locations in various states of decay and disrepair. While the urban explorers are the human storytellers, they are simply interpreting what the land has revealed.

"Stories of course must have a place to live, so places become characters," Ben Logan wrote in his book *The Land Remembers*.[82] He continues, "The land outlives us all, forever remembering us and writing an epitaph for the good or evil we do to it."[83]

Part of the abuse of abandoned buildings may be due to certain people's thrill of destroying property that they're not responsible for cleaning up. It also appears to be part of our human nature to always desire more items and bigger and better everything, especially when it comes to buildings, technology, and physical posses-sions. As conservationist and environmentalist Aldo Le-opold wrote in his book, *A Sand County Almanac and Other Writings on Conservation and Ecology*, "We abuse land because we regard it as a commodity belonging to us. When we see land as a community to which we belong, we may begin to use it with love and respect."[84]

From watching The Proper People's videos, I've determined most buildings are typically abandoned for one of the following reasons: (1) A newer, bigger building was constructed as a replacement; (2) a business collapsed, and the owners simply left nearly everything behind; or (3) the technology housed in the building has become obsolete, and the location is no longer needed (e.g., power plants).

Most of the time, when I watch The Proper People's videos, I feel disappointed at how quickly buildings can go into disrepair when they are not taken care of properly. Most of the videos involve hotels, theaters, and hospitals that are literally damaged from the top down. Water from a leaky or highly damaged roof can quickly cause mold and moisture to build that cause ceiling tiles to fall, metal to rust, paint to peel, and plaster to crumble. I'm also disheartened when videos reveal piles of paperwork and clearly confidential information left behind. We need to use our resources wisely, perform regular building maintenance, and consider the impact of construction types. Like The Proper People have shown us, **observations identify opportunity** to make positive change through environmental stewardship projects.

Reflection Questions
1. Who is ultimately responsible for caring for aban-doned buildings—commercial or residential—in your community?
2. What's the best way to discard items in an environ-mentally sustainable way?
3. What projects have you noticed that are positively impacting the environment?

Action Items
1. Check with your local municipality what items can be recycled.
2. Work with area organizations to create secure drop-off locations to properly discard paperwork, electronics, and medications.
3. Donate items you no longer need or use to area or-ganizations that will benefit people in need.

CHAPTER 20

Everything is Connected

Duke Welter grew up on a lake in northern Wisconsin. He loved to walk along the shore and explore. When he was eight years old, he got to operate his own fishing boat with a 5.5-hp motor. He enjoyed fishing and later learned the craft of fly-fishing for trout. Welter would check the trout's gullet and stomach to see what they were eating to keep track of the health of the fish and to develop a home waters fly box. His lifelong hobby led him to explore western Wisconsin, where he noticed many streams had a troublesome layer of thick sediment.[85] As a part of Trout Unlimited, a national nonprofit organization focused on protecting and restoring streams, Welter proposed the Driftless Area Restoration Effort (DARE), a project that restored streams and provided a healthy habitat for trout and other wildlife.[86]

The Driftless Area is a unique region in the Upper Mississippi River basin that includes 42 counties in southeastern Minnesota, southwestern Wisconsin, northeastern Iowa, and northwestern Illinois. Glaciers bypassed the area, leaving unique limestone and sandstone formations in the form of bluffs and many rivers and streams. In the early 1800s, naturalists and geologists who explored the area noticed the absence of glacial drift—the boulders and gravel left behind when glaciers

recede—and referred to the region as the Driftless Area.
To many, the area is an ideal trout-fishing destination,
especially in April and May.

As Welter explained, at the time of European settle-
ment, hundreds of spring creeks were rich with brook
trout. However, the way early settlers used the land in the
1840s through the 1900s was detrimental to those
streams and their natural habitat.

"They logged off the hillsides, they plowed uphill
and down, and they didn't worry about soil erosion,"
Welter explained. "Eventually, they lost soil up on the
ridgetops and the hillsides. This went into the valleys. So
all over the region they have the same kind of problem—
a thick blanket of sediment on valley floors and less rich
soil left on the hillsides."

In the 1930s, conservationist and environmentalist
Aldo Leopold and a team from the U.S. Soil Erosion Service (now part of the Natural Resources Conservation
Service) and the University of Wisconsin–Madison College of Agriculture (now the College of Agricultural and
Life Sciences) worked on the Coon Creek Watershed
Project, which tried to lessen soil erosion and flooding
problems in the Driftless Area.[87] Leopold said the federal
bureau, in cooperation with many farmers in the area,
used all possible remedial methods to save land by building concrete check dams in gullies, terracing fields, planting alfalfa or clover, planting slopes in alternating strips

following the contour, curbing cows and sheep, and planting trees.[88]

Trout Unlimited's DARE project expanded on Leopold's and other conservationists' work over the years by focusing on stream restoration. The project, which was formally announced in 2005, included a collaborative effort with four states and a proclamation from the U.S. Department of Agriculture that the project was an environmental priority for federal and state agencies. One of the project features included adjusting vertical banks to a four-to-one slope instead of a two-to-one slope. That way, it's a wider, gentler slope around the stream to stabilize the soil and prevent flooding, and to keep farmers from losing corn as streamside banks erode.

Volunteers were also involved in other important conservation projects. From 1983 to 2013, Welter and volunteers built and created about 10,000 lunker structures, a man-made structure that provides trout with overhead cover from the sun and protection from predators. Volunteers later made more natural habitats using boulders and installed root wads and rock weirs. They also planted more long-lived, durable shade trees around streams. Welter estimated about $65 million has been spent on the Driftless Area restoration in the last 20 years. There's now about 1,500 miles of publicly accessible healthy streams to fish compared to about 700 miles prior to the project.

"I drew a 30-mile radius from my front door and re-alized I had 30–40 really good streams to fish," Welter said. "And I don't think I've fished them all yet."

People who fish, hunt, and hike may be considered the first line of environmental protection. They are more intimately engaged with the environment and may be the first to notice things that need attention. Observations create opportunity to make positive change through en-vironmental stewardship projects. We need to be a wit-ness to the land's history, listen to ideas to make improve-ments, and have the foresight to predict how changes will have an impact. Decisions humans made in the past and ones we'll make in the future have a direct impact on the overall well-being of our environment and commu-nity. **Everything is connected.** We need to remember, attend to, and anticipate the needs of the land in differ-ent geographical areas.

"We're not at a place where we can clap our hands together and say, 'Nice job! Let's go have a beer. It's done,'" Welter said. "It's an ongoing challenge."

Reflection Questions
1. How do you care for the environment?
2. What environmental challenges does your community face?
3. In what ways do you enjoy the natural beauty in your area?

Action Items
1. Join an organization that is dedicated to environmental stewardship projects.
2. Research an environmental stewardship project in a different area of the country.
3. Go for a walk on a nearby trail. Be observant of the natural beauty and take note when you return to see if it remains the same of if a path starts to deteriorate.

CHAPTER 21

We Need Mentors

Every year, registered robotics teams across the United States receive a package from FIRST®—For Inspiration and Recognition of Science and Technology—that includes an exciting video that describes a new game they'll play for six weeks in competition. They also receive an intense 120-page rulebook that describes the limitations of the robots students build for competition. Every team dreams about competing at a high level and making it to the national championship, but that's not the main goal of robotics. It's about progress, perseverance, and personal growth. Students achieve those goals with guidance from their coaches.

Mark Moulton is the coach of Team 2977—the Sir Lancer Bots, an extracurricular high school robotics program in La Crescent, Minnesota. The team was one of five founding members of the 7 Rivers Robotics Coalition, a nonprofit organization in the Coulee Region focused on providing access and opportunities to learn science, technology, engineering, and mathematics (STEM) skills through robotics organizations. Mark has served as the executive director of the coalition for several years. Each school year, Mark and his wife, Kristi, who is also an educator, interview students as part of the team recruitment process. They want to make sure students understand the time and energy they'll need to commit to the team, and provide them with opportunities to develop their communication skills. Robotics is about individual and team achievement in design, problem solving, programming, building, marketing, and communication.

"I love watching kids go through the learning process, figuring out different approaches and concepts that make their robot function and play the FIRST® game as best as possible," Mark said.[89]

Most of the students who were a part of Team 2977 in the past have pursued a STEM career path after high school. For example, Zach travels and maintains robotic milkers for mass-production dairy farms; Chris works with IBM's Watson and artificial intelligence; and Jason earned a doctorate in quantum computing. However, not everyone who shows interest in robotics pursues it as a career.

When a student joined the team as a freshman, he displayed a drive and determination to be a programmer, having never tried it before. Over time, the student realized he didn't really like programming. He shifted to a marketing role before telling Mark he was quitting the team.

"I feel like I failed you," the student, with tears in his eyes, regrettably told Mark.

"No, you didn't," Mark quickly responded.

He reassured the student that, from his perspective as a coach, he actually succeeded. The student was able to explore a career path early in life, identified areas of interest, had the courage to speak up, and moved forward on a more passionate path.

That student now works at a hospital in Seattle.

"We don't always know the effect we have on kids until later on," Mark said as a coach and teacher.

Several students who graduated have returned to mentor students and play a significant role in running the team.

"I think part of mentorship is the 'pass it on' mentality," Mark said. "I think that is one way an organization can grow."

Dedicated mentors provide a safe and supportive space for people to be creative, make mistakes, and explore options. **We need mentors** in life, whether it's for just a short time, a season, or a lifetime.

Reflection Questions
1. Who have served as mentors in your life?
2. How have mentors helped you with projects or supported your passion?
3. Who have you helped guide as a mentor?

Action Items
1. Explore mentorship program possibilities at your organization.
2. Identify options in your community where you can be a mentor.
3. Reconnect with one of your mentors and thank them for the ways they helped shape your career or provided personal guidance.

CHAPTER 22

Create More Leaders

When he was 15 years old, Elliott Schroeder wanted to work so he could buy a car. He was hired at a locally owned Culver's, a Wisconsin-based fast-food franchise. Schroeder started as an entry-level crew member, working the register and serving customers.[90]

"One time, I had a funny experience," Schroeder said. "I spilled a huge bag of ketchup on the floor in the dining room. The leader at the time just stayed really calm. It could just be her demeanor, but it's also part of this book called *Extreme Ownership*. For me, the lesson is detaching from your emotions in stressful situations, stepping back, and making the right call."[91]

Schroeder read that book as part of a leadership development program at Culver's. A mentor at that restaurant encouraged him to apply to the program three months into working there.

While the Culver's franchise provides basic information on running a shift, customer satisfaction, and team building, individual restaurant owners are encouraged to implement their own leadership program. Jake and Emily Bowe own and operate two Culver's locations in Onalaska, Wisconsin, and one in Winona, Minnesota. They created a multilevel program that incorporates Culver's management lessons and expands upon them to focus on the growth and development of leaders. The Bowes want to **create more leaders** not only to continue to run a successful business, but to help build community and a supportive culture. It all starts with an application and individual initiative. Applicants need to answer questions such as the following: *What are your strengths? What do you need to know for this role? Why do you want to do this job?*

"To me, one of the key aspects of being a great leader is being able to reflect and to be able to say, 'Hey, this is where I went wrong and I'm going to try something different,'" Jake said.[92]

The Bowes want to help people build on their strengths, identify knowledge gaps, and find solutions to problems.

"It's real easy to sit and say, 'This is wrong and that's wrong,'" Jake said. "It's much harder to get somebody to say, 'This is wrong. Here are some thoughts on how to make it better. Here are some thoughts on what we should do next.'"

As they progress through the program, leaders at different levels are trained on a variety of increasingly complex situations, ranging from how to answer certain types of phone calls, to how to respond to guest complaints, to how to take donations. Leaders participate in extensive role-plays related to customers, team members, and vendors. That's in addition to participating in a leadership book review with a small group and meeting one-on-one monthly with a mentor. Schroeder still remembers a particular instance when a mentor at Culver's in Onalaska helped him be a better leader.

One late night after work, Schroeder was waiting for his parents to pick him up. His supervisor sat next to him. Schroeder had been grumpy during his shift, wishing he were at home visiting with his family's houseguests rather than working.

"Hey, I just noticed you weren't your normal self today," she told him.

He was impressed that she noticed and would even mention it at 11 p.m., after their shift had ended and her work was done. Not wanting to give too much detail, he simply responded he felt out of it that day. She kindly said that sometimes you just have to put on a smile and do your best.

"It's almost a fluff type of advice, but I find it to be very true, and it always stuck with me," Schroeder said.

When he advanced through the leadership program to become the team lead in the kitchen, Schroeder recalled her advice. He had established a routine that helped him be more present and energized at work. He put on his signature necktie, made sure his apron was on tight, and greeted his teammates.

"It was like putting on this extra persona," Schroeder said. "Not being fake, but adding an extra level of 'this is me when I'm at work.' I'm energized. I'm showing love to the people in the kitchen. I want to be proud of the work we do."

Schroeder worked part-time at Culver's for about four years. When he returned to work during college breaks, he was always curious to see how others had progressed through the leadership program. He was impressed by the culture of growth and how leaders encouraged the team members to take more responsibility and make an investment in themselves. Schroeder was also able to make an investment by purchasing his first vehicle, a 2005 Buick LeSabre Limited, which he is still proud to own today.

Reflection Questions
1. What are your strengths?
2. How do you create a culture of growth at home or at your organization?
3. What book has had a positive impact on your life?

Action Items
1. Describe a situation in which a leader encouraged you or provided constructive feedback.
2. Explore leadership training program(s) at your organization.
3. Propose a community conversation on leadership development.

CHAPTER 23

Bye Bad Bosses

My boss gathered several office supplies. Following my simple direction, he wrote BELIEVE in blue lettering on a yellow piece of paper. He attached blue tape to all four sides. He started to place the sign above our office door, but I stopped him.

"It needs to be slightly tilted."

He made an adjustment without question.

"Perfect," I said.

My boss, Dillon McArdle, had not seen *Ted Lasso*, the popular Apple TV+ show. He listened intently when I explained the importance of the BELIEVE sign at our Viterbo University Fine Arts Center team potluck. Ted Lasso, the show's title character, is an American college football coach who was hired to be the head coach of a beloved but struggling football team in England. Ted did not know much about football (soccer), but he was incredible at character development. At the beginning of his coaching tenure, he placed a small yellow sign with BELIEVE written in blue lettering above his office door in the locker room. He huddled his team during halftime of a tied game.

"Fellas, we're broken," he said. "We need to change."[93]

At the end of his speech, he grabbed their attention one last time.

"Hey, hey, hey, one last thing. And I want everyone's eyes on me when I say this. Look at me." He then slapped the BELIEVE sign above the doorway and went into his office. It was the beginning of the team coming together and believing they could accomplish their goals.

Dillon was the first to slap our new office sign. Several others followed, including myself. The BELIEVE sign stayed up for years, and a second version was added across the room with a team photo when Dillon was named employee of the year. Of course, it takes way more than just slapping a sign on a wall to make a positive work environment that's welcoming, inclusive, and safe—both physically and psychologically. Servant leaders like Dillon and Ted understand the importance of getting to know their team and making sure they feel supported in different ways. They practice their deep listening skills, make observations, and assist as needed so their team grows personally and professionally. Servant leaders do all of this while moving the organization's mission and vision forward.

Unfortunately, we don't always work for servant leaders. While the people and circumstances vary, bad bosses tend to share similar characteristics. Self-serving leaders care about privilege, power, and prestige. They prioritize decisions that build themselves up and may tear others down. Sometimes bosses are not very competent in their role, but they can learn and grow. Sometimes they are negligent. Other times, they are malicious and micromanage, erode trust, and cause cultural damage. They tend to focus on profits over people and may lose sight of their organization's mission and vision. Self-serving leaders tend to keep information close to their chest and may share limited or inaccurate information to different people or groups. They may also misuse power to yell at or degrade employees as an intimidation tactic. They may allow you to talk to your colleagues, but only about work and nothing personal. While bad bosses may say they are open to constructive feedback, they likely are not and may become resentful to those who actually give their opinion. Working for a bad boss may make you cynical and irritable and cause you to lose your drive and determination—at least temporarily. You can, and you will, feel better. It will just take some time, self-reflection, and usually a change of scenery.

I've learned that people and institutions may break your heart, but you can't let them break your spirit. So, what are your options if you're working in a toxic culture or dealing with a bad boss? You can initially raise red flags and provide constructive feedback, but that usually does not work or only gets you so far. Direct reports have two options when dealing with a bad boss: leave or wait them out. From my experience, it's best to leave. Waiting out a bad boss will be more painful because you will pay the price for their misdeed(s). They won't feel the same pain. *Eventually* they will fail, but it might not be the way you think, and sometimes they take the organization down with them. It will take several years for an organization to rebuild culture and recover a team from a bad boss, especially because those who remain have been hired and conditioned a certain way. It will be difficult to reset the tone, rebuild trust, and create new expectations and experiences.

If you decide to stay and wait out the bad boss, you can try to distance yourself as much as possible and cut back your organizational involvement, such as respectfully removing yourself from a nonessential committee. Be sure to keep your receipts, or make sure everything is in writing when incidents occur. The biggest battle will be mental. You have to keep hope alive. You have to imagine how much better it could be and how you want to feel at work. You could seek out others who have gone through similar circumstances and ask how they felt after they made a big change. And you should start applying elsewhere.

Pay, purpose, and people are three things that tend to keep a person at a job. In general, when you have a safe work environment and a servant leader as a boss, you will likely feel happier, be more engaged, and have an increased sense of self-worth. Servant leaders must make sure people's needs are met and work to build an inclusive, supportive, and safe community. They can accomplish this with active listening, accepting constructive feedback, taking concerns seriously, making ethical decisions, and considering different ways to solve problems. Servant leaders are empathetic and enthusiastic. We're human, though, so there will be moments when we all mess up and say or do something upsetting. That's where forgiveness and problem solving come in. And so does the tilted BELIEVE sign, as no one is perfect.

"There's two buttons I never like to hit, alright?" Ted said during a news conference. "And that's panic and snooze."[94]

I have definitely wanted to hit both of those buttons throughout my career. But when I have a servant leader, a positive work environment, and a strong and trustworthy team, I feel most like myself. I feel like I do not need to worry about getting yelled at for whatever reason, and I am able to do more than the status quo. We can learn a lot from fictional and real servant leaders in our lives. The biggest lesson they can teach us is about establishing trust and maintaining it. If you don't trust your team and they don't trust you, you can't lead effectively. Trust is the hardest thing to rebuild. We have to find the strength to say **"bye bad bosses"** when that trust is eroded beyond repair.

Reflection Questions
1. What are some traits of a good boss?
2. How can you tell the difference between a servant leader and a self-serving leader?
3. How have you processed a past situation involving a bad boss?

Action Items
1. Write an apology letter to yourself from a bad boss. Then destroy it. Discuss how you felt during this process.
2. Create a list of events that have been disadvantageous for you. Next to each one, write what you learned and how you were able to move forward.
3. Review your organization's policy for reporting a negative situation/incident. Identify areas that should be updated or alternate methods that should be created for people who may not feel comfortable reporting to a direct supervisor.

CHAPTER 24

Light the Candle

There was an unexpected knock on Daniel's office door. A young, charismatic Black woman stood in the doorway.

"So you're the new voice teacher," she said. "Can I see how you breathe?"

"Okay," Daniel said while welcoming her into his office.

The woman put her hand on his diaphragm and paid close attention.

"That was my introduction to Sister Thea," Daniel said with a laugh, remembering his friend of nearly 20 years.[95]

Daniel Johnson-Wilmot was a young music faculty member at Viterbo College (later University) when he met Sister Thea Bowman in 1973. She started teaching English there the prior school year. At one point in their friendship, Sister Thea gave him the title of "Little Brother." They talked about work, music, civil rights issues, and personal experiences. He had met her parents and felt like a member of the family.

At age 15, Sister Thea, who was born Bertha Bowman, left her home in Canton, Mississippi, to begin her journey as one of the Franciscan Sisters of Perpetual Adoration (FSPA) in La Crosse, Wisconsin. Sister Thea was the only African American member of her religious community. Her grandfather was a slave.[96] Sister Thea earned a bachelor of arts in English from Viterbo, which was founded by the FSPA in 1890. The FSPA's mission is to be a "community of vowed Franciscan women centered in Eucharist, committed to being a loving presence through prayer, witness, and service."[97] Whether she was teaching or being a witness and testifying, Sister Thea always found a way to lift people up, encourage them to embrace their identity, and use their gifts to the best of their ability.

"I was taught to do my best, try my hardest, and keep striving up the ladder," Sister Thea said. "But at each rung I was to reach back and help a brother, sister, or stranger receive the gift and pass it on and thus help create a more caring, sharing world."[98]

Sister Thea started her teaching career with fifth and sixth grade at a Catholic school in La Crosse and later taught English and vocal music at a high school in Canton.[99] Several years later, Sister Thea's FSPA superiors asked her to complete a doctorate so she could return to Viterbo and teach English. She earned a master's degree and doctorate in English from the Catholic University of America and started teaching English at Viterbo in the fall of 1972. She soon became the department chair and formed the Hallelujah Singers, a gospel chorale.

"Thea used the Socratic method," Johnson-Wilmot said. "You talked in class. You didn't get by without participating. Everything was participatory education. She told me one time, 'If there's no pain, there's no gain.' If there's no struggles in learning, you're not learning anything."

Sister Thea encouraged students to use their whole body in their presentations to capture attention and show emotion. She was proud of her African American heritage, especially related to song, dance, and cultural traditions. She worked toward racial equality. In 1989, Sister Thea gave an address at the U.S. Conference of Catholic Bishops, where she explained the struggles of Black communities in the Catholic Church and in the United States. She said people did not feel at home, struggled to gain access to equal opportunities, and lacked basic necessities.[100]

Sister Thea gave her memorable speech to the U.S. bishops while being treated for breast cancer. She was diagnosed in 1984, the same year her parents, Dr. Theon (a physician) and Mary Esther (a teacher), passed away. Sister Thea understood her physical limitations, persevered through pain, and carried on as best as she could with help from others.

Near the end of her life, Sister Thea's "Little Brother" and several Viterbo students went to her house to visit. Johnson-Wilmot had led a group down to Canton for a choir concert trip. Sister Thea was thankful to hear such joyful music in her home when students sang for her, yet she further encouraged them to show more emotion and allow the music to move them.

"Let your light shine," she would tell students. "Each one, teach one. Walk your talk."[101]

Sister Thea died at the age of 52 on March 30, 1990. Her "Little Brother" helped prepare the church for her funeral, which was packed.

"I was always blown away by what she did even though I knew her so well," Johnson-Wilmot said. "To see her in action was unbelievable. She had a way of pulling people into a story and thought process. She had the power of a saint, which goes beyond what a pope or bishop or archbishop have. She created that power by herself. She wasn't commissioned somewhere."

And by power, Johnson-Wilmot was not talking about control; he was talking about an invitation. Sister Thea invited people to listen to a story, to understand a perspective, and to learn something new. She called herself a little "rowdy."[102] Sister Thea was blunt, yet spoke the truth with love. She was bold, yet found a diplomatic way to speak from the heart.[103] She came to the U.S. bishops, her community leaders, her students, and her friends as a messenger. In November 2018, the U.S. bishops endorsed the sainthood cause for canonization of Sister Thea. At the time of this writing, the process is still ongoing.

At times, we may find ourselves overwhelmed by the many problems in the world. The darkness can overshadow all the good things happening. Sister Thea's grandfather was a slave, she saw the challenges Black communities experienced, and she was diagnosed with cancer the same year her parents died. And yet with all of that grief, she still found hope and worked toward making the world a more loving place.

"I think one difference between me and some other people is that I'm content to do my little bit," Sister Thea said. "Sometimes people think they have to do big things in order to make change. But if each one of us would **light the candle**, we'd have a tremendous light."[104]

Reflection Questions
1. What teacher(s) inspired you?
2. How do you encourage others to embrace their identity and use their gifts?
3. In what way did something small you did or witness make a big difference in someone's life?

Action Items
1. Speak the truth with love to someone important in your life.
2. Write a note to a teacher and tell them how much you learned from them.
3. Explore a time in your life where you needed light to guide you and how it helped.

CHAPTER 25

Just Keep Growing

Jonah Larson was such a "rascal" when he was young that he made his daycare providers and teachers question their career path. He threw shoes and pencils, ripped up his classmates' projects, stole snacks and ate them in the bathroom, removed ceiling panels, and poured a can of paint on the floor to create his own Slip 'N Slide.[105] At one point, Jonah's parents asked his educators to stop giving him behavioral slips because they thought he was collecting them. He already had 57, and the school year wasn't over. Luckily, Jonah's "rascal years" would dwindle thanks to a teacher who redirected his energy, a compassionate mentor in the medical field, and an opportunity to turn his craft into an early career.

When he was a baby, Jonah was found wrapped in a bundle of false banana leaves along a dirt path in Durame, a village in Ethiopia. At about six months old, he was adopted by Jennifer and Christopher Larson from La Crosse, Wisconsin. The orphanage had given them a few photos of Jonah from the months they took care of him. Years later, when his family more closely analyzed those photos and the ones of him being bottle-fed at home, they noticed Jonah's eyes would look away from the person feeding him. They also later found out that he wasn't held as often as babies need during his first six months because there were so many children in the orphanage. Jonah also had an intense desire to be with his mom, Jennifer, in his early childhood development, doing nearly anything to be with her.

The Larson family later learned Jonah's lack of eye contact and his behavior problems were symptoms of reactive attachment disorder (RAD). This realization came thanks to Dr. Jeff Thompson, then-CEO of Gundersen Health System and a retired pediatrician, and a team of compassionate health care providers. During Jonah's rascal years, his mom worked as an administrator at Gundersen. Dr. Thompson was her mentor. He was aware of the many times she needed to leave work to get Jonah from school due to behavioral problems. Dr. Thompson was kind and understanding. He would invite Jonah to hang out in his office. In addition to mentoring his mother, Dr. Thompson became someone Jonah could confide in. He once received a video from Jonah wishing him a happy new year and confessing, "I did something very wrong"; in the video, Jonah further explained how he would make it up to the classmate he had wronged. He even shared his new year's resolution: "to have a ton of sympathy for other people." He then expressed hope that Dr. Thompson would also follow through on his new year's resolution, whatever it may be.

When Jonah was five years old, his aunt brought a bag of leftover craft supplies to his house. He found "a shiny, pointy tool" (crochet hook) and a ball of yarn. His mom found a YouTube video on how to make a dish-cloth, which Jonah completed within an hour, "the first of thousands of crochet items I would make over the next 10 years." He then went on to learn advanced skills from watching YouTube videos. Jonah's fifth-grade teacher encouraged him to work on his crochet instead of throwing pencils once he had finished his schoolwork. As of this writing, Jonah is 17 years old. He has been featured in *Forbes*, *Oprah Daily*, and *The Times* (of London).[106] He's had film crews from Poland, Germany, and New Zealand come to his house. He's also been featured in stories in China and Russia. He has been a kid correspondent on *The Drew Barrymore Show* and won the inaugural episode of the HBO Max show *Craftopia*.[107] His flower crochet bag will be on display as part of an exhibit in the Smithsonian American Art Museum in Washington, DC, for about a year, starting August 2025.

Jonah is also an author and an entrepreneur with his own line of craft kits and a foundation—Jonah's Hands—that benefits kids in the Ethiopian village where he was born. His foundation, in partnership with Roots Ethiopia, has built a school library (Jonah's Library) with 3,000 books, restrooms, and a science lab and equipment, and employed an award-winning teacher.

"The ripple effect of your giving is enormous," Dr. Thompson told Jonah.[108]

Part of Jonah's giving back is thanks to the promise his parents made with his orphanage. At the farewell ceremony, they said, "Don't let him forget where he came from." The desire to serve others also comes from his parents and family. His dad told him, "Wealth is not a prerequisite of generosity."

Being human is complicated. We all have things we've said or done that we're not proud of or that have brought other people down instead of lifting them up. We can learn and grow from our mistakes. We can ask for forgiveness. We can better understand how our past impacts our present. We can learn to be more compassionate toward ourselves and more empathetic toward other people's challenges. Servant leaders make sure people's needs are met and they continue to grow in different ways, both personally and professionally.

Jonah hopes his rascal years are behind him, but it's partly because of them that he's become the person he is today. He has a strong desire to serve others and make things better. He plans to continue his craft and potentially go into the medical field. When asked what his hope is for the future, Jonah paused and said, "I just want to do my part and help others as much as I can. Obviously, I can't do everything. I can't fix all wrongs. But I can change a lot." **Just keep growing.**

Reflection Questions
1. In what ways have you grown in your personal or professional life?
2. What do you need to continue to learn and grow?
3. When were you quick to judge someone when you should have been more compassionate about what they were possibly going through?

Action Items
1. Identify a time in your life when you had to make a change for the better and the steps you had to take.
2. Contact a person who helped you through a challenge in your life and reconnect.
3. Ask for forgiveness and give yourself grace.

Afterword

My high school swim coaches taught me, "Leave it better than you found it." If our section of the swim pool at a meet was messy when we arrived, we cleaned up the area before we left. The first couple of times we threw away other people's trash, I was annoyed. I didn't leave the mess, so why should I have to clean it up? But then I thought about how I would want the pool area to look—clean and tidy not just for us but for others who use the space. I also wanted our home pool deck and locker room to be clean and tidy to show we cared about our team, our guests, our community, and our resources. My coaches were teaching me more than how to be a stellar swimmer. They were teaching me about community and how to lead by example.

There are various ways servant leaders can show we care about people in our lives—personally and professionally. The biggest thing we can do is to create a healthy and safe environment—physically and psychologically—that allows people to be themselves and provides opportunities for them to learn and grow. We have to establish, build, and maintain trust. We must also make ethical decisions that are in the best interest of the people we serve. It takes practice. It's hard work. And it's the work of a community.

The 25 lessons in this book represent a fraction of the diverse stories that can be told to exemplify the practicality and importance of servant leadership. More stories can be told about how people achieve success and inspire others to follow and build strong communities. More stories can be told about people making a difference across the United States and world, especially when it comes to environmental sustainability projects. More stories can also be told about how personal passions have led people to certain professions and a desire to serve. What impacts us personally impacts us professionally, and vice versa.

Servant leaders should be observant, curious, and trustworthy. They should also be contemplative and creative and do things with integrity. Leaders should inspire people to do their best, give them grace to learn from their mistakes, and provide opportunities to engage in system redesigns. Servant leaders should also be good stewards and look at the big picture. Servant leaders should have a growth mindset, lift others up, and find ways to create more healthy leaders. While all of that can be overwhelming and challenging at times, it can also be rewarding and fulfilling. In order to do this noble work for the common good, we need to **just keep growing**.

Blessing for Leaders

By Martha Boehm

May you look for patterns.
Patterns that identify complex problems.
Patterns that solve system glitches.
Patterns that prevent future issues.

May you sit with grief.
Grief that comes from loss.
Grief that comes from change.
Grief that comes from experience.

May you experience pure joy.
Joy that comes from laughter.
Joy that comes from storytelling.
Joy that comes from the heart.

May you care for people.
People with different abilities.
People with different backgrounds.
People with different talents.

May you always keep learning.
Learning about your team.
Learning about your strengths.
Learning about your virtues.

May you just keep growing.

Acknowledgements

First of all, thank *you* for reading this book! You have thousands of messages coming at you every day. I'm humbled you chose to read the stories I've written about individuals who are learning and growing every day— just like you. I hope you are able to find your own Top 5 Takeaways and move the lessons forward in your personal and/or professional life.

Thank you to all of the individuals featured in this book, especially the ones who took time out of their busy schedule to talk about an important part of their life with me. I hope you find you are in good company in this book, surrounded by people who want the best for their family, friends, and community.

Thank you to my master of arts in servant leadership professors Rick Kyte and Tom Thibodeau for reminding me to focus on my strengths, be an ethical big-picture thinker, and let my light shine as a spirit carrier. Rick, thank you for introducing me to your Four-Way Method for Ethical Decision Making, for being my colloquium project advisor, and for helping me expand that project into this book. Tom, thank you for your vulnerability, your wise words, and your seemingly endless ways of encouraging me and building my confidence.

Thank you to my master's program cohort and students outside the program who took classes with me. I appreciated all of the generative questions and deep conversations we had during the program and after we earned the degree. Thank you to Gwen Schroeder for your faith-filled suggestions and insight. Thank you to Sophia Woychik for your encouragement and your gift of active listening.

Thank you to my teammates at the Viterbo University Fine Arts Center, especially my "work wife" Rachel Frisby. I hope you all continue to BELIEVE in your good, creative work long after that *Ted Lasso*–inspired sign is gone from the wall.

Thank you to Amber Field for being a beta reader and providing constructive feedback and encouragement. Thank you to Kristi Moulton for initial cover idea discussions. Thank you to Deb Kappmeyer for cover design consultation. Thank you to Melinda Masson for proof reading.

And thank you to all of my supportive friends and family, especially my husband, Brandon Furlano. Brandon, I appreciate seeing you lead by example. I also appreciate you listening to all of my stories and puns. Thank you for your love and support!

Notes

PREFACE
[1] Robert K. Greenleaf, *Servant Leadership: A Journey into the Nature of Legitimate Power and Greatness* (Paulist Press, 1977), 27 [italics in the original].
[2] Greenleaf, *Servant Leadership*, 27 [italics in the original].
[3] Greenleaf, *Servant Leadership*, 188 [italics in the original].

CHAPTER 1: GO BEYOND TRANSACTIONS
[4] Dave Skogen in discussion with the author, October 10, 2022.
[5] Dave Skogen, *Boomerang! Leadership Principles That Bring the Customer Back* (9th Street Publishing, 2013), xxiii.
[6] Horst Schulze with Dean Merrill, *Excellence Wins: A No-Nonsense Guide to Becoming the Best in a World of Compromise* (Zondervan, 2019), 33–37.

CHAPTER 2: STORIES REVEAL PURPOSE
[7] Tom Thibodeau in discussion with the author, February 14, 2023. All of Thibodeau's quotes that follow come from this conversation.
[8] Herbert Anderson and Edward Foley, *Mighty Stories, Dangerous Rituals: Weaving Together the Human and the Divine* (Fortress Press, 2019), 3.

CHAPTER 3: RITUALS ARE POWERFUL

[9] "Po Atarau" ("Now Is the Hour"), composed by Clement Scott, arrangement and lyrics by Maewa Kaihau and Dorothy Stewart, first recorded by Ana Hato with Deane Waretini in 1927, released as track 18 on *He Puiaki Puoru Treasures in Sound*, Kiwi, 1995. This song was made internationally popular by Gracie Fields and later Bing Crosby.

[10] Paul Woodruff, *Reverence: Renewing a Forgotten Virtue* (Oxford University Press, 2014), 6.

[11] Woodruff, *Reverence*, 15.

[12] Tom Thibodeau, in discussion with the author, March 12, 2022.

CHAPTER 4: CELEBRATE THIRD PLACES

[13] "Under the Sea," composed by Alan Menken, lyrics by Howard Ashman, from the album *The Little Mermaid: Original Motion Picture Soundtrack* (Walt Disney Records, 1989).

[14] The Weber Center for the Performing Arts is home to La Crosse Community Theatre and a performance site for Viterbo University.

[15] Ray Oldenburg, *Celebrating the Third Place: Inspiring Stories About the "Great Good Places" at the Heart of Our Communities* (Marlowe & Company, 2001), 2.

[16] Robert D. Putnam, *Bowling Alone: The Collapse and Revival of American Community*, 20th anniversary ed. (Simon & Schuster, 2020), 416.

[17] Putnam, *Bowling Alone*, 367.

CHAPTER 5: SPHERE OF INFLUENCE

[18] The song "La Que Manda," written by Gina Chávez and Andrea Corona, was released on May 27, 2020. It was produced, engineered, and mixed by Adrian Quesada and Gina Chávez at Electric Deluxe Recorders.

[19] Gina Chávez, in discussion with the author, October 27, 2023. All quotes that follow are from this conversation.

CHAPTER 6: BEGIN WITH GOOD

[20] Arbender Robinson, "Dreams Do Come True," conference presentation, Viterbo University Conference on Servant Leadership, La Crosse, WI, July 1, 2022.

[21] *Hairspray*, book by Mark O'Donnell and Thomas Meehan, lyrics by Scott Wittman and Marc Shaiman, music by Marc Shaiman, dir. Jack O'Brien, chor. Jerry Mitchell, Neil Simon Theatre, July 18, 2002–January 4, 2009.

[22] *The Book of Mormon*, book, lyrics, and music by Robert Lopez, Trey Parker, and Matt Stone, dir. Trey Parker and Casey Nicholaw, chor. Casey Nicholaw, Eugene O'Neill Theatre, February 24, 2011–present.

[23] *Les Misérables*, book by Alain Boublil and Claude-Michel Schönberg, lyrics by Herbert Kretzmer, music by Claude-Michel Schönberg, dir. Laurence Connor and James Powell, Imperial Theatre, March 1, 2014–September 4, 2016.

[24] "About Arbender," Arbender Robinson, accessed November 16, 2022, https://www.arbender.com/bio.

[25] Robinson, "Dreams Do Come True."

[26] Amit Sood, MD, "Resilient Living Part Two, Dr. Amit Sood," presentation, November 8, Viterbo University (as

part of the D.B. Reinhart Institute for Ethics in Leadership annual lecture series), posted April 9, 2020, by Richard Kyte, YouTube, 21:56, https://youtu.be/jSV_JGVQjBY.

[27] "The morning pages" is a concept by author Julia Cameron in her book *The Artist's Way: A Spiritual Path to Higher Creativity*, 25th anniversary ed. (Tarcher, 2016), 9–18.

CHAPTER 7: HAVE COURAGEOUS CONVERSATIONS

[28] Dean Dickinson, in discussion with the author, December 13, 2022. All Dickinson quotes that follow are from this conversation.

[29] Richard Kyte, *An Ethical Life: A Practical Guide to Ethical Reasoning* (Anslem Academic, 2012), 17.

[30] Kyte, *Ethical Life*, 183.

CHAPTER 8: REACH COMMON UNDERSTANDING

[31] Phil Rosenthal, host, *Somebody Feed Phil*, documentary series, season 4, episode 2, "The Mississippi Delta," Netflix, October 30, 2020.

[32] Rosenthal, "Mississippi Delta."

[33] Joe Furlano, in discussion with the author, June 27, 2022.

[34] Rosenthal, "Mississippi Delta."

CHAPTER 9: EXPLORE VARIOUS SOLUTIONS

[35] Mark Schack, in discussion with the author, August 7, 2023. All of Shack's quotes that follow come from this conversation.

[36] Richard Kyte, *An Ethical Life: A Practical Guide to Ethical Reasoning* (Anselm Academic, 2012), 66.

[37] Kyte, *Ethical Life*, 65.

[38] Kyte, *Ethical Life*, 65.

[39] Schack initially learned of Kyte's Four-Way Method to Ethical Decision Making in Kyte's ethics class as part of Viterbo University's master of arts in servant leadership program. Schack earned that degree in 2013.

CHAPTER 10: GO GLITCH HUNT

[40] Linda W. Belton, in discussion with the author, December 5, 2022. All of Belton's quotes that follow come from this conversation.

[41] Belton first introduced glitch hunts versus witch hunts in her book *A Nobler Side of Leadership: The Art of Humanagement: A Servant Leader Journey* (Greenleaf Center for Servant Leadership, 2016). She then expanded on the concept into systems thinking in *The Intentional Servant Leader: Premise and Practice: A Symphony of Service* (Greenleaf Center for Servant Leadership, 2018).

CHAPTER 11: WE EXPERIENCE LIFEQUAKES

[42] Cleveland Clinic, "Commotio Cordis," accessed October 14, 2023, https://my.clevelandclinic.org/health/diseases/24572-commotio-cordis.

[43] Bruce Feiler, *Life Is in the Transitions: Mastering Change at Any Age* (Penguin Press, 2020), 94-95.

[44] Feiler, *Life Is in the Transitions*, 79.

[45] "Micah Hyde and Damar Hamlin: 'Staying Ready' | Buffalo Bills," posted October 1, 2023, by Buffalo Bills, YouTube, 6:54, https://youtu.be/-VKLKg4uR20?si=b3lGPxqF2vON5fQn.

[46] Chasing M's Foundation, "Damar Hamlin Announces Youth Football Camp, Community Events and Chasing M's Foundation CPR Tour in Pittsburgh," June 29, 2023, https://www.chasingmsfoundation.com/upcoming-events/chasing-ms-foundation-cpr-tour-in-pittsburgh.

[47] Feiler, *Life Is in the Transitions*, 162–63.

CHAPTER 12: WE SHARE HOPE

[48] Ayan shared her story with James A. Bowey who included it as part of his presentation, "We Can Walk Together: Embracing the Stranger in Divided Times," at the Viterbo University Conference on Servant Leadership, La Crosse, WI, July 1, 2022.

[49] The poem "Ayan, 2016" is reprinted with permission from James A. Bowey.

[50] James A. Bowey, in discussion with the author, December 20, 2024. All quotes from Bowey that follow are from this conversation.

CHAPTER 13: ON YOUR HEART

[51] Reuters, "Florida Is So Cold Iguanas Are Falling Out of Trees," NBC News, January 31, 2022, https://www.nbcnews.com/news/amp/rcna14167.

[52] Sister Sarah Hennessey, Franciscan Sisters of Perpetual Adoration, trained to be a spiritual director at Spiritual Directors International.

[53] Sister Sarah Hennessey, in discussion with the author, July 21, 2023. All quotes that follow are from this conversation.

CHAPTER 14: HUMOR CAN HEAL

[54] Lisa David Olson, in discussion with the author, August 12, 2023.

[55] ABC News, "Humor Helps Carol Burnett Cope," June 12, 2002, accessed August 13, 2022, https://abcnews.go.com/2020/story?id=123891&page=1.

[56] Lisa provides more details about her love of Carol Burnett and the role she played in her life in her book *Laughs on Wry: An Improviser's Memoir* (Comedy Alley, 2018). She has also spoken at TEDx events.

[57] Mayo Clinic Staff, "Stress Relief from Laughter? It's No Joke," September 22, 2023, https://www.mayo-clinic.org/healthy-lifestyle/stress-management/in-depth/stress-relief/art-20044456.

[58] Lisa loves to take a #SeriousSelfie. She has a series of photos with strangers as a way of building connection and community in addition to having a little fun.

[59] I do not live in Indiana, but it was good to know they could deliver there.

CHAPTER 15: REPURPOSE YOUR TOOLS

[60] Carolyn Colleen, *F.I.E.R.C.E.: Transform Your Life in the Face of Adversity, 5 Minutes at a Time!* (CreateSpace Independent Publishing Platform, 2016).

[61] Colleen, *F.I.E.R.C.E.*, 15 [italics in the original].

[62] Carolyn Colleen, in discussion with the author, August 3, 2023. All quotes from Colleen that follow are from this conversation.

[63] Colleen, *F.I.E.R.C.E.*, 55–56. Reprinted with permission from Carolyn Colleen.

[64] Robert K. Greenleaf, *Servant Leadership: A Journey into the Nature of Legitimate Power and Greatness* (Paulist Press, 1977), 27 [italics in the original].

[65] United Nations Commission on the Status of Women, accessed August 29, 2023, https://www.un-women.org/en/csw.

CHAPTER 16: RETHINK THE SITUATION

[66] Natalie Jankowski, in discussion with the author, September 12, 2023. All of Jankowski's quotes that follow are from this conversation.

[67] Natalie notes there has been advancement in medical technology. Now most scoliosis surgeries use titanium.

[68] Adam Grant, *Think Again* (Viking, 2021), 211.

[69] Natalie also sought the assistance of a physical therapist to help her hips, as one was slightly higher than the other due to scoliosis.

[70] Jeff Galloway recommends switching between running and walking at timed intervals to reduce fatigue, recover

quicker, and reduce core body temperature. "Run Walk Run: It Began in 1974," accessed September 13, 2023, https://www.jeffgalloway.com/training/run-walk/.
[71] Grant, *Think Again*, 28.

CHAPTER 17: TAKE A WALK

[72] Stephanie Ross, in discussion with the author, September 8, 2023.
[73] Manoush Zomorodi, *Bored and Brilliant: How Spacing Out Can Unlock Your Most Productive and Creative Self* (St. Martin's Press, 2017), 5.
[74] Zomorodi, *Bored and Brilliant*, 5.
[75] Richard Louv, *The Nature Principle: Reconnecting with Life in a Virtual Age* (Algonquin Books of Chapel Hill, 2011), 3.

CHAPTER 18: FIND MORE AWE

[76] Ethan Reed, in discussion with the author, September 7, 2023. All of the quotes from Reed that follow are from this conversation. Reed worked on Chandu's design with three others; he created the final design for the sculpture.
[77] Dacher Keltner, *Awe: The New Science of Everyday Wonder and How It Can Transform Your Life* (Penguin Press, 2023), 249.
[78] Keltner, *Awe*, 18.

CHAPTER 19: OBSERVATIONS IDENTIFY
OPPORTUNITY

[79] "Abandoned Asylum with Power—How Does This Still
Work!?," posted April 26, 2019, by The Proper People,
YouTube, 34:40, https://youtu.be/sCssyRYfYw8.

[80] The Proper People, YouTube, joined May 26, 2014,
https://www.youtube.com/TheProperPeople.

[81] Michael and Bryan do not reveal their last names for pri-
vacy reasons.

[82] Ben Logan, *The Land Remembers: The Story of a Farm
and Its People* (University of Wisconsin Press, 1975), 293.

[83] Logan, *Land Remembers*, 302.

[84] Aldo Leopold, *A Sand County Almanac and Other Writings on Ecology and Conservation*, ed. Curt Meine (Library of
America, 2013), 4.

CHAPTER 20: EVERYTHING IS CONNECTED

[85] Duke Welter, in discussion with the author, February 1,
2023. All quotes from Welter that follow are from this conversation.

[86] Duke Welter was a newspaper journalist and lawyer by
trade. After he retired from lawyering, he spent 12 years as
Trout Unlimited's DARE outreach coordinator. He retired
from that role in 2022.

[87] Aldo Leopold, *A Sand County Almanac and Other Writings on Ecology and Conservation* (Library of America, 2013),
363.

[88] Leopold, *Sand County Almanac*, 363.

CHAPTER 21: WE NEED MENTORS

[89] Mark Moulton, in discussion with the author, September 5, 2021. All quotes that follow are from this conversation.

CHAPTER 22: CREATE MORE LEADERS

[90] Elliott Schroeder, in discussion with the author, February 10, 2023.

[91] See Jocko Willink and Leif Babin, *Extreme Ownership: How U.S. Navy SEALs Lead and Win* (St. Martin's, 2017).

[92] Jake Bowe, in discussion from the author, February 6, 2023. Bowe is a graduate of Viterbo University's master of arts in servant leadership program.

CHAPTER 23: BYE BAD BOSSES

[93] *Ted Lasso*, season 1, episode 5, "Tan Lines," written by Brett Goldstein, directed by Elliot Hegarty, aired August 28, 2020, on Apple TV+.

[94] *Ted Lasso*, season 2, episode 1, "Goodbye Earl," written by Brendan Hunt, directed by Declan Lowney, aired July 31, 2021, on Apple TV+.

CHAPTER 24: LIGHT THE CANDLE

[95] Daniel Johnson-Wilmot, in discussion with the author, December 7, 2022. All quotes from Johnson-Wilmot that follow are from this conversation.

[96] Viterbo University, "Biography and Legacy of Sr. Thea Bowman," accessed December 11, 2022, https://www.viterbo.edu/sr-thea-bowman-center/biography-and-legacy-sr-thea-bowman.

[97] Franciscan Sisters of Perpetual Adoration, "Mission and Vision," accessed December 11, 2022, https://www.fspa.org/content/about/mission-modern-lives.

[98] Celestine Cepress, ed., *Sister Thea Bowman, Shooting Star: Selected Writings and Speeches* (Saint Mary's Press, 1993), 17.

[99] Cepress, *Sister Thea Bowman*, 24–25.

[100] Cepress, *Sister Thea Bowman*, 31.

[101] Cepress, *Sister Thea Bowman*, 25.

[102] Johnson-Wilmot, in discussion with the author.

[103] Johnson-Wilmot, in discussion with the author.

[104] Sister Thea Bowman, interview by Mike Wallace, *60 Minutes*, CBS, May 3, 1987.

CHAPTER 25: JUST KEEP GROWING

[105] Jonah Larson, "Jonah's Hands," presentation at the Viterbo University Conference on Servant Leadership, La Crosse, WI, June 30, 2023.

[106] Rachel Kramer Bussel, "11-Year-Old Boy Lands Book Deal About Crocheting After His Creations Go Viral," *Forbes*, February 26, 2019, accessed February 23, 2025, https://www.forbes.com/sites/rachelkramer-bussel/2019/02/26/jonah-larson-crochet-book-deal/; Shelly Copeland, "Jonah Larson, a 12-Year-Old Crochet Prodigy, Will Bring You Pure Joy," *Oprah Daily*, July 16, 2020, accessed February 23, 2025, https://www.oprahdaily.com/life/a33262498/jonah-larson-crochet/; Barbara McMahon, "Meet the Crochet Kid Jonah Larson: An Instagram Sensation," *The Times*, June 8, 2019,

accessed February 23, 2025,
https://www.thetimes.com/uk/social-media/article/meet-the-crochet-kid-jonah-larson-an-instagram-sensation-rnvg38qxv.

[107] *The Drew Barrymore Show*, season 2, episode 24, "Meredith Hagner/Jonah Larson/Patti Peck," written by Cristina Kinon, Chelsea White, and Elizabeth Koe, directed by Adam Heydt, aired October 14, 2021, on CBS; *Craftopia*, season 1, episode 1, "It's My Party and I'll Craft If I Want To," directed by Adam Sampson, aired May 27, 2020, on HBO Max.

[108] Jeff Thompson supported Jonah on stage during "Jonah's Hands," his presentation at the Viterbo University Conference on Servant Leadership, La Crosse, WI, June 30, 2023.

Further Reading

Anderson, Herbert, and Edward Foley. *Mighty Stories, Dangerous Rituals: Weaving Together the Human and the Divine*. Fortress Press, 2019.

Belton, Linda W. *A Nobler Side of Leadership: The Art of Humanagement*. The Greenleaf Center for Servant Leadership, 2016.

Belton, Linda W. *The Intentional Servant Leader: Premise and Practice*. The Greenleaf Center for Servant Leadership, 2018.

Cameron, Julia. *The Artist's Way: A Spiritual Path to Higher Creativity*, 25th anniversary ed. TarcherPerigee, 2016.

Cepress, Celestine, ed. *Sister Thea Bowman, Shooting Star: Selected Writings and Speeches*. Saint Mary's Press, 1993.

Colleen, Carolyn. *F.I.E.R.C.E.: Transform Your Life in the Face of Adversity, 5 Minutes at a Time*. CreateSpace Independent Publishing Platform, 2016.

David Olson, Lisa. *Laughs on Wry: An Improviser's Memoir.* Comedy Alley, 2018.

Feiler, Bruce. *Life Is in the Transitions: Mastering Change at Any Age.* Penguin Press, 2020.

Grant, Adam. *Think Again: The Power of Knowing What You Don't Know.* Viking, 2021.

Greenleaf, Robert K. *Servant Leadership: A Journey into the Nature of Legitimate Power and Greatness.* Paulist Press, 1977.

Keith, Kent M. *Servant Leadership at Work: Caring About People and Getting Extraordinary Results.* Terrace Press, 2024.

Keltner, Dacher. *Awe: The New Science of Everyday Wonder and How It Can Transform Your Life.* Penguin Press, 2023.

Kyte, Richard. *An Ethical Life: A Practical Guide to Ethical Reasoning.* Anselm Academic, 2012.

Kyte, Richard. *Finding Your Third Place: Building Happier Communities (and Making Great Friends Along the Way).* Fulcrum, 2024.

Leopold, Aldo. *A Sand County Almanac and Other Writings on Ecology and Conservation.* Library of America, 2013.

Logan, Ben. *The Land Remembers: The Story of a Farm and Its People.* University of Wisconsin Press, 1975.

Louv, Richard. *The Nature Principle: Reconnecting with Life in a Virtual Age.* Algonquin Books of Chapel Hill, 2011.

Nutt, Maurice J., ed. *Thea Bowman: In My Own Words.* Liguori Publications, 2009.

Oldenburg, Ray. *Celebrating the Third Place: Inspiring Stories About the "Great Good Places" at the Heart of Our Communities.* Marlowe & Company, 2001.

Putnam, Robert. *Bowling Alone: The Collapse and Revival of American Community*, 20th anniversary ed. Simon & Schuster, 2020.

Schulze, Horst, with Dean Merill. *Excellence Wins: A No-Nonsense Guide to Becoming the Best in a World of Compromise.* Zondervan, 2019.

Skogen, Dave. *Boomerang! Leadership Principles That Bring the Customer Back.* 9th Street Publishing, 2013.

Thompson, Jeff. *Lead True: Live Your Values, Build Your People, Inspire Your Community.* ForbesBooks, 2017.

Woodruff, Paul. *Reverence: Renewing a Forgotten Virtue.* Oxford University Press, 2014.

Zomorodi, Manoush. *Bored and Brilliant: How Spacing Out Can Unlock Your Most Productive and Creative Self.* St. Martin's Press, 2017.

About the Author

Martha Boehm loves a good story, especially one that is uplifting or inspirational. She is curious, creative, and contemplative. She began her career in local TV news as a reporter/videographer, producer, and digital content manager. After six years as an award-winning journalist, she shifted her focus to communications and marketing, and leadership development. She received a Servant Leader Award from Viterbo University, where she earned a master of arts in servant leadership. She also earned a master of arts in media studies and a bachelor of arts in journalism and mass communication from the University of Wisconsin–Milwaukee. Besides stories, she finds inspiration from traveling, theater, and sports. She lives in Wisconsin with her husband, Brandon.

About the Cover

This book's cover image features a photo taken by Martha Boehm from part of the Heian-jingu Shrine garden in Kyoto, Japan. Filters have been applied to make the image appear like a painting. The author chose this cover image partly for her appreciation of Japanese culture, which focuses on humans and nature living in harmony. The stepping stones across the pond are named Garyu-kyo, or "hidden dragon bridge." The stones were repurposed from pillars that supported old bridges. The author also chose this image because the journey of a servant leader isn't straightforward or simple; there are many uneven—and sometimes rocky—paths that provide opportunities to learn and grow as we take steps forward.

www.ingramcontent.com/pod-product-compliance
Lightning Source LLC
Chambersburg PA
CBHW021156130626
46554CB00005B/1838